# BREAD MACHINE COO

A COMPLETE AND EASY BAKIN

WITH **301** QUICK RECIPES TO PREPARE

YOUR HOMEMADE BREAD, INCLUDING

TIPS AND TRICKS FOR A BETTER

FINAL PRODUCT AND TO SAVE MONEY

## MARIE JEFFERSON

# Introduction

Even if you are not good at using modern appliances, leave your worries behind. Bread machines have simple and user-friendly controls and using them is fun and easy!

Bread is an everyday staple. A food item we regularly purchase, buying store-bought bread is undoubtedly convenient. However, store-bought bread is packed with chemical additives, extra sugars and salts to ensure longer shelf life. To gauge how baking your own bread is worth it, do yourself a favor; look at the label on the back of store-bought bread and compare it to the list of ingredients needed to make your own. You will notice the stark contrast of ingredients. Store-bought includes emulsifiers and agents, but a basic bread recipe is made up of very few affordable ingredients, none of which include words that I even struggle pronouncing. And when you look at the bigger picture, you'll see you are better off baking your own bread, especially with quite a convenient and useful tool, such as a bread machine.

There are many pros to making bread at home, including the fact that it is far tastier than your standard, mass-produced bread. You can alter ingredients, meaning you have more control over the sugar, fiber, Protein: and salt content. You can also get inventive by adding in nuts and dried fruits. Buying your own ingredients means you can manage all of what goes in the machine and provides you the opportunity of seeking the freshest ingredients.

**Advantages of Bread Machines**

**A bread machine does it all instead of you**. This means you will be able to avoid kitchen mess, as the bread machine does everything from mixing to kneading to baking. Yes, it sounds like magic, but it is for real. Just imagine warm bread and a clean kitchen. Dreams can come true!

**Bread machines keep your health under control**. By this, we mean that you can choose the ingredients you want and create a bread that is carb-free and free of any additives that might cause harm to your body. This feature is very appreciated by those who follow the keto diet. You can make your own bread that is much better than the store-bought version, at a low cost, and you know it was created in a clean environment where cross-contamination is not possible.

**A bread machine allows you to have fresh, warm bread every day**. This is perhaps the most obvious benefit of a bread-making machine. Most bread machines have a time function you can set to have your bread ready at a certain time. This is very useful, as it allows you to prepare the ingredients and then continue with your daily chores, while the bread machine does everything else for you. Just imagine, you are coming home after an exhausting day of work, and warm, delicious bread is waiting for you!

**Bread machines save money**. Yes, bread machines may be expensive initially, but buying bread every day, or even just every week, is more costly. Not to mention all of that thrown away bread, the stale bread that no one wants to eat anymore. With each slice, you are throwing away your money. The bread machine maker allows you to make smaller or larger loaves and ones that fit your family's dietary and consumption habits. Besides, making bread from scratch is always cheaper than buying it at the store.

**Bread machines produce better quality bread**. Fresh bread is fresh bread, and no store-bought version can compete with that. In addition, what about that chewy, rubber-like bread you sometimes get? Something like that will never happen to you with a bread-making machine. The homemade bread is made with natural ingredients and does not have any artificial additives. The additives that are used in store-bought bread can keep it fresher for a longer time, but they affect the texture. It is always better to make bread fresh and additive-free than to eat "fake-fresh" bread for days.

**Bread machines are easy to use.** The bread machine looks like a simple appliance, and believe us, it is. If you are not good with the baking process and somehow you always end up with over- or under-cooked foods, you can skip this worry, as the bread-making machine bakes everything to perfection.

**Bread making machines make more than bread.** The bread machine can be used for many other purposes besides making bread. You can use it to make a baguette, sweet breads, and even dough. The possibilities are endless.

These are just some of the advantages of a bread machine. We are sure you will soon discover others and learn to appreciate the many uses of a bread machine. And while that happens, we suggest you enjoy our recipe collection from this book.

# Chapter 1.    How A Bread Machine Is Made In General

Bread is a baked food that can be set up from various kinds of batter. The mixture is ordinarily made of flour and water. The sizes and types of flour and the different fixings change, as do the laying techniques. From the beginning, bread was one of the most basic foods, as well as one of the most established counterfeits. Certainly, people have been making bread since the beginning of horticulture.

Bread is typically arranged from wheat flour mixture, which is made with yeast and permitted to rise. Normally, individuals heat bread in the stove. In any case, an ever-increasing number of individuals go to the extraordinary bread machines to prepare crispbread at home.

## What Is A Bread Machine?

A bread machine is a kitchen appliance for heating bread. The gadget is a shovel or bread tin, made in the spatulas, which is located in the center of a small multifunctional original mesh.

## How Is Bread Machine Made?

This machine is essentially a conservative electric appliance that holds a solitary, huge bread tin inside. The tin itself is somewhat extraordinary – it has a hub at the base that is associated with an electric engine underneath.

A little metal oar is appended to the pivot at the base of the tin. The oar is answerable for manipulating the mixture. A waterproof seal secures the hub itself. We should investigate every one of the bread machine parts in detail:

- The top over the bread producer comes either with the survey window or without it

- The control board is likewise situated on the highest point of the bread machine with the end goal of comfort

- In the focal point of the top, there is a steam vent that depletes the steam during the heating procedure. A portion of the bread creators likewise have an air vent on the gadget for air to come inside the tin for the mixture to rise

## Benefits of a Bread Machine

While utilizing a bread machine for some may seem like a pointless advance, others don't envision the existence without newly home-heated bread. In any case, how about we go to the realities – underneath, we indicated the advantages of owning a bread machine.

As a matter of first importance, you can appreciate the crisply prepared handcrafted bread. Most bread creators additionally include a clockwork, which permits you to set the preparing cycle at a specific time. This capacity is extremely valuable when you need to have sweltering bread toward the beginning of the day for breakfast.

You can control what you eat. By preparing bread at home, you can really control what parts are coming into your portion. This choice is extremely valuable for individuals with sensitivities or for those, who attempt to control the admission of a fixings' portion.

It is simple. A few people believe that preparing bread at home is chaotic, and by and large, it is a hard procedure. In any case, preparing bread with a bread machine is a breeze. You simply pick the ideal choice and unwind - all the blending, rising, and heating process is going on within the bread producer, which additionally makes it a zero chaos process!

It sets aside your huge amounts of cash in the long haul. If you imagine that purchasing bread at a store is modest, you may be mixed up. In turns out that in the long haul, preparing bread at home will set aside your cash, particularly in the event that you have some dietary limitations.

Incredible taste and quality, you have to acknowledge it – nothing beats the quality and taste of a crisp heap of bread. Since you are the person who is making bread, you can ensure that you utilize just the fixings that are new and of a high caliber. Homemade bread consistently beats locally acquired bread as far as taste and quality.

## How Does Bread Machine Work?

To begin with, you put the plying paddle inside the tin. At the point when the tin is out of the machine, you can gauge the fixings and burden them into the tin.

A while later, you simply need to put the skillet inside the stove (machine), pick the program you wish by means of the electronic board, and close the top. Here the bread producer enchantment dominates!

One of the main things the bread machine will do is working the batter – you will hear the sounds. On the off chance that your bread creator accompanies the preview window, you can watch the entire procedure of preparing, which is very interesting.

After the massaging stage, everything will go calm for quite a while – the rising stage comes. The machine allows the mixture to dough and rise. At that point, there will be another round of manipulating and a period of demonstrating.

Although the typical bread making process is programmed, most machines accompany formula books that give you various intriguing propelled bread plans.

The best thing about using a bread-making machine is it gets the hard cycle of bread making easy. You can use the bread-making machine in complete cycle, especially for loaf bread, or you can just do the dough cycle if you are baking bread that needs to bake in an oven. To use the bread-making machine, here are some steps to guide you:

*Familiarize yourself with the parts and buttons of your bread-making machine*

Your bread-making machine has three essential parts, and without it, you will not be able to cook your bread. The first part is the machine itself, the second is the bread bucket, and the third is the kneading blade. The bread bucket and kneading blade are removable and replaceable. You can check with the manufacturer for parts to replace it if it's missing.

Learn how to operate your bread-making machine. Removing and placing the bread bucket back in is important. Practice snapping the bread bucket on and off the machine until you are comfortable doing it. This is important because you don't want the bucket moving once the ingredients are in place.

*Know your bread bucket capacity*

This is an important step before you start using the machine. If you load an incorrect measurement, you are going to have a big mess on your hand. To check your bread bucket capacity:

- Use a liquid measuring cup and fill it with water.
- Pour the water on the bread bucket until it's full. Count how many cups of water you poured on the bread bucket.

The number of cups of water will determine the size of your loaf bread

- Less than 10 cups =1-pound loaf

- 10 cups =1 to 1 ½ pounds loaf

- 12 cups=1 or 1 ½ to 2 pounds loaf

- 14 cups or more=1 or ½ to 2 or 2 ½ pounds loaf

*Learn the basic buttons and settings of your bread-making machine.*

Here are some tips you can do to familiarize yourself with the machine:

- Read all the button labels. The buttons indicate the cycle in which your machine will mix, knead, and bake the bread.
- Basic buttons include START/STOP, CRUST COLOR, TIMER/ARROW, SELECT (BASIC, SWEET, WHOLE WHEAT, FRENCH, GLUTEN FREE, QUICK/RAPID, QUICK BREAD, JAM, DOUGH.)

- The SELECT button allows you to choose the cycle you want in which you want to cook your loaf. It also includes DOUGH cycle for oven-cooked breads.

## *Using the Delay button*

When you select a cycle, the machine sets a preset timer to bake the bread. For example, if you select BASIC, time will be set by 3 hours. However, you want your bread cooked at a specific time, say, you want it in the afternoon, but it's only 7:00 in the morning. Your bread cooks for 3 hours, which means it will be done by 10:00 am, but you want it done by 12. You can use the up and down arrow key to set the delay timer. Between 7 am and 12 noon, there is a difference of 5 hours, so you want your timer to be set at 5. Press the arrow keys up to add 2 hours in your timer so that your bread will cook in 5 hours instead of 3 hours. Delay button does not work if you are using the DOUGH cycle.

## *Order of adding the ingredients*

This only matters if you are using the delay timer. It is important to ensure that your yeast will not touch any liquid so as not to activate it early. Early activation of the yeast could make your bread rise too much. If you plan to start the cycle immediately, you can add the ingredients in any order. However, adding the ingredients in order will discipline you to do it every time and make you less likely to forget it when necessary. To add the ingredients, do it in the following order:

- First, place all the liquid ingredients in the bread bucket.

- Add the sugar and the salt.

- Add the flour to cover and seal in the liquid ingredients.

- Add all the other remaining dry ingredients.

- Lastly, add the yeast. The yeast should not touch any liquid until the cooking cycle starts. When adding the yeast, make a small well using your finger to place the yeast to ensure proper timing of yeast activation.

## *Using the Dough Cycle*

You cannot cook all breads using the bread-making machine, but you can use the machine to make the bread-making process easier. All bread goes under the dough cycle. If your bread needs to be oven-cooked, you can still use the bread-making machine by selecting the DOUGH cycle to mix and knead your flour into a dough. To start the Dough cycle:

- Add all your bread recipe ingredients in your bread bucket.

- Select the DOUGH cycle. This usually takes between 40 to 90 minutes.

- Press the START button.

- After the cycle is complete, let your dough rest in the bread-making machine for 5 to 40 minutes.

- Take out the dough and start cutting into your desire shape.

Some machines have various Dough cycle, which you can use for muffin recipes. However, if all you have is basic dough setting, you can use it for muffin recipe, but you need to stop the machine before the rising cycle begins.

## How to use a bread machine

Even if you're not good at using modern appliances, put your worries behind you, because bread machines have simple, easy-to-use controls. They are fun and easy to use! Besides making fresh bread, they can also make and knead any type of dough, bake dough out of the box, and even make dough jam. When you get to know this handy device, it will truly become an essential and exceptional aid in your kitchen.

It's so simple

Insert the baking sheet into the machine.

Attach the dough blades.

Add ingredients as shown in your machine manual.

Close the lid.

Turn on the machine.

Select the required function.

What Else Can It Do?

Different bread machines may differ in their design, capacity, number of accessories, and programs available. When choosing your bread machine, think of your own preferences and needs: What will you do with the machine? Do you need any particular programs and additional modes, or is the basic functionality enough?

Bread machines can knead the dough, let it rest, bake a crunchy baguette, make sweet cupcakes or unleavened bread, and much more.

# Chapter 2.  What Are The Most Common Ingredients

Bread making consists of a few very basic ingredients flour, liquids, yeast, butter, etc. Knowing the role of these ingredients helps you to understand the baking process. Moreover, the order in which you add ingredients is crucial when making bread in your bread machine. Do not commit the cardinal sin of bread making by adding the ingredients randomly to the bread pan.

The following sections highlight the correct order to put ingredients in the bread pan to bake perfect loaves of bread.

## Water/Milk

All of the other basic bread ingredients, including flour, salt, and yeast, need a liquid medium to do their respective tasks. Water is the most common liquid ingredient; milk, buttermilk, cream, and juice are some common substitutes.

The liquid is usually the first ingredient to be added to the bread pan. This is very important as it maintains the ideal texture of your bread. The liquid should not be cold; ensure that it is lukewarm (between 80 and 90°F) whenever possible.

### Butter/Oil

Butter, oil, or fat is usually added after the liquid. This is what gives bread crust its attractive brown color and crispy texture. Do not use cold butter that has just been taken out of the refrigerator. You can either microwave it for a few seconds or keep it at room temperature until it gets soft.

### Sugar/honey (if using)

Sweet ingredients such as honey, corn syrup, maple syrup, and sugar are usually added after the butter as they mix easily with water and butter. However, the sweetener can be added before the butter as well. Sugar, honey, etc. serve as a feeding medium for yeast, so fermentation is stronger with the addition of sweet ingredients.

### Eggs (if using)

Eggs need to be at room temperature before they are added to the bread pan. If the eggs are taken from the refrigerator, keep them outside at room temperature until they are no longer cold. They keep the crust tender and add protein and flavor to the bread.

### Chilled Ingredients

If you are using any other ingredient that is kept chilled, such as cheese, milk, buttermilk or cream, keep it outside at room temperature until it is no longer cold, or microwave it for a few seconds to warm it up.

### Salt

Use table salt or non-iodized salt for better results. Salt that is high in iodine can hamper the activity of the yeast and create problems with fermentation. Furthermore, salt itself is a yeast inhibitor and should not be touching yeast directly; that is why salt and yeast are never added together or one after another.

### Spices (if using)

Spices such as cinnamon, nutmeg, and ginger are often used to add flavor to the bread. They may be added before or after the flour.

## Flour

Flour is the primary ingredient for any bread recipe. It contains gluten (except for the gluten-free flours) and protein, and when the yeast produces alcohol and carbon dioxide, the gluten and protein trap the alcohol and carbon dioxide to initiate the bread-making process.

There are many different types of flours used for preparing different types of bread. Bread machine flour or white bread flour is the most common type as it is suitable for most bread recipes. It's so versatile because it contains an ideal proportion of protein for bread baking.

Usually, flour is stored at room temperature, but if you keep your flour in your fridge, allow it to warm up before using it.

## Seeds (if using)

If a recipe calls for adding seeds such as sunflower seeds or caraway seeds, these should be added after the flour. However, when two different flours are being used, it is best to add the seeds in between the flours for a better mix.

## Yeast

Yeast is the ingredient responsible for initiating the vital bread-making process of fermentation. Yeast needs the right amount of heat, moisture and liquid to grow and multiply. When yeast multiplies, it releases alcohol and carbon dioxide.

You can use active dry yeast or bread machine yeast (both will be available in local grocery stores). Cool, dry places are ideal to store yeast packs.

Yeast is added to the bread pan last, after the flour and other dry ingredients. (For certain types of bread, like fruit and nut bread, yeast is technically not the last ingredient, as the fruits or nuts are added later by the machine. However, yeast is the last ingredient to be added before starting the bread machine.)

# Chapter 3.    Some Suggestions About Ingredients

**F**lour, yeast, water, and salt work together to form the bread.

**Let's start with the flour.** It is an entire world but, to simplify things a little, we will say that it is nothing more than the result of the grinding of a cereal, seed, or tuber. The most common flours for baking are wheat flour (there are many varieties of this cereal); oats; corn; rye; barley and even nuts like chestnut. It is fundamental to know the behavior of this basic ingredient since the result of the dough will be very different according to the grinding and the cereal used. As the flour that is used more frequently is that of wheat, we will focus on it (although without stopping - for now - in its varieties).

In general terms, we could say that **wheat flour is composed of starch and other elements (in variable proportions) such as minerals, vitamins, proteins, and ashes.** The sifting of the milling influences these factors. The whole grain, keeping the bran, make up the whole flours; if they are deprived of it, we will obtain white flours. There are flours of soft wheat and durum wheat, the difference of these lying in the amount of protein that each contains and, therefore, the result of the bread will be different.

The proteins (gliadin and glutenin) that are in the flour are the main things responsible for the formation and elasticity of the dough that, together with the fermentation, makes the bread have volume and consistency. As the flour is hydrated, the proteins bind, transforming into gluten. When we manipulate a bread dough, and they are oxygenated, the dough becomes elastic and workable. If the mass is well hydrated and kneaded, a protein mesh (glutinous network) is created that covers it. The more protein the flour has, the more water it will need, so you must be careful not to overdo it.

**Yeast is the second** great protagonist of bread. Typically, a fungus is used (suitable for ingestion), which can be found in two versions: dry (lyophilized) or fresh. Keep in mind that this latest version is a living organism, so it must be appropriately conserved, as it loses strength over time. If dry is used, the proportion of yeast is 1/3 of the amount indicated in the recipe for fresh. For example, if it calls for 10 gr. of fresh yeast, you should use 3 gr. of dry yeast.

Another way to produce bread is the use of natural sourdough, the oldest way to make the bread ferment (through bacteria that are present in the environment). When the bread is made with sourdough, it usually has a slightly acidic taste, lasts longer, has an intense smell, and, due to bacterial fermentation, facilitates digestion. The process of making the sourdough is simple, but it takes time (it usually takes about 5 days). Here you have a good recipe.

**Water and salt** have no major complications and secrets. It must be made clear that it is not necessary to use mineral water; tap water works perfectly even if some prefer to filter it. In fact, in the best professional bakeries, no water other than tap water is used. Salt brings flavor, and you can use several types of salts (marine, with herbs, etc.). In fact, the bread doesn't have to have salt; many loaves are traditionally bland, and others are brushed with a saline solution when leaving the oven (especially the loaves with little crumbs).

**Flour, yeast, water, and salt** are all the essential ingredients you need to make a good bread dough. Before carrying it to the oven comes the work of fermentation, kneading, etc. But as a useful note (and to encourage you to make bread), we must remember that not all the loaves are baked, nor do they need many hours of fermentation and kneading.

There is the bread that can be made in **a pan, griddle, casserole, or steamed**, and are an excellent option for when you do not want to heat the oven. You can also make many other pieces of bread in skillets, such as pita bread, Moroccan bread, bread from North Africa, and a variety of flatbreads. Making bread in a pan is one of the eldest ways of cooking it. If you decide to make bread in the pan, you must choose a good one that keeps the heat well and can cook evenly.

# Chapter 4.    Tips And Tricks In Order To Have A Better Final Product And To Save Money And Time

When you are using a bread machine for the first time, it's common to have some concerns. However, they are quite easy to fix. The following are some useful tips and quick-and-easy fixes for the most common problems encountered while baking bread in a bread machine.

## Dough Check

You can check the progress of the dough while the bread machine is mixing the ingredients. Take a quick check after 5 minutes of kneading. An ideal dough with the right amount of dry and wet ingredients makes one smooth ball and feels slightly tacky. You can open the lid to evaluate the dough. Do not worry about interfering with the kneading process by opening the lid; the bread structure won't be affected even if you poke it to get a feel for the dough.

If the dough feels too wet/moist or does not form into a ball shape, you can add 1 tablespoon of flour at a time and check again after a few minutes. If you feel that the dough is too dry, or it has formed two or three small balls, you can add 1 teaspoon of water at a time and check again after a few minutes.

## Fruit/Nut Bread

When making fruit or nut bread, it is very important to add fruits or nuts at the right time. Not all bread machines come with a nut/fruit dispenser or hopper. If yours doesn't have one, don't worry; the machine will signal you with a beep series when it's time to add the fruits or nuts.

## Citrus Ingredients

Citrus ingredients such as lemon zest, orange zest, orange juice, lemon juice, and pineapple juice can create issues with yeast fermentation if added in excess. Do not add more than the quantity specified in a recipe. The same goes for alcohol and cinnamon.

## Salt Adjustment

When making small loaves (around 1 pound), sometimes the loaf rises more or less than expected. In many such instances, the issue is with the quantity of salt added. To avoid problems, try using less salt or cutting back on the quantity specified in the recipe. Using sea salt or coarse salt can also help prevent problems with small loaves.

## Bread Collapse

The amount of yeast is very important for proper rising. The most common reason for bread collapse during the baking process is adding too much or too little yeast. Do not add more yeast than specified in the recipe. Also, check the expiration date on the yeast pack; freshly packed yeast provides the best results. Other reasons for bread collapse are using cold water and adding excess salt.

## Failure to Rise

Many factors can contribute to the failure of dough to rise completely. Insufficient gluten content, miscalculated ingredients, excess salt, excess sugar, and using cold ingredients are the most common reasons. Always warm any chilled ingredients or place them at room temperature for a while before adding them to the bread pan. However, if you are warming any ingredients in your oven, make sure not to overheat them. They need to be lukewarm, at between 80 and 90°F, and not too hot. Also make sure that the yeast does not come in direct contact with the salt, as this creates problems with rising (that is why yeast is added last).

## Texture Troubles

- If your bread has a coarse texture, try adding more salt and reducing the amount of liquid.

- If your bread looks small and feels dense, try using flour with higher protein content. Bread flour has a sufficient amount of protein, but slightly denser loaves are common when you use heavier flours such as rye flour and whole wheat flour. Use additional ingredients such as fruits, nuts, and vegetables in their specified quantities. Adding too much of such ingredients will make your loaf too heavy, small, and dense.

- Moist or gummy loaves are less common, but it can happen if you have added too much liquid or used too much sugar. Too much liquid can also result in a doughy center.

- If your bread has an unbrowned top, try adding more sugar. This can also happen if your bread machine has a glass top.

- If your loaf has a mushroom top, it is probably due to too much yeast or water. Try reducing the amount of water and/or yeast.

- Sometimes a baked loaf has some flour on one side. When you bake the next time, try to remove any visible flour during the kneading cycle with a rubber spatula.

- If your loaf has an overly dark crust, try using the Medium crust setting next time. This also happens if you've added too much sugar and when you fail to take out the bread pan after the end of the baking process. It is always advisable to remove the bread pan right after the process is complete.

- If your loaf has a sunken top, it is probably because of using too much liquid or overly hot ingredients. This is also common during humid or warm weather.

**Excess Rise**

Many times, a loaf rises more than expected; the most common reasons are too much yeast, too little salt, and using cold water. But also make sure that the capacity of your bread pan is sufficient for the size of loaf you have selected; trying to make a large loaf in a small bread pan will obviously lead to such trouble.

**Paddles**

After the bread machine completes its baking process the paddles may remain inside the bread loaf. Allow the freshly made bread to cool down and then place it on a cutting board and gently take out the paddles.

Spraying the paddles with a cooking spray before you add the ingredients to the bread pan will make it easier to clean them after the bread is baked.

**Cleaning**

After you take the baked loaf from the bread pan, do not immerse the pan in water. Rather, fill it with warm soapy water.

# Chapter 5.  Basic Bread

## 1. Basic White Bread

**Preparation Time:** 1 hour 15 minutes

**Cooking Time:** 50 minutes (20+30 minutes)

**Servings:** 1 loaf

**Difficulty:  Easy**

**Ingredients:**

- ½ to 5/8 cup Water
- 5/8 cup Milk
- 1 ½ tablespoon butter or margarine
- 3 tablespoon Sugar
- 1 ½ teaspoon Salt
- 3 cups Bread Flour
- 1 ½ teaspoon Active dry Yeast

**Directions:**

1   Put all ingredients in the bread pan, using minimal measure of liquid listed in the recipe.

2   Select medium Crust setting and press Start.

3   Observe the dough as it kneads. Following 5 to 10 minutes, in the event that it seems dry and firm, or if your machine seems as though it's straining to knead, add more liquid 1 tablespoon at a time until dough forms well.

4   Once the baking cycle ends, remove bread from pan, and allow to cool before slicing.

**Nutrition:**

Calories: 64 Cal

Fat      : 1 g

Carbohydrates: 12 g

Protein : 2 g

## 2. Gluten Free Bread

**Preparation Time:** 4 hour 50 minutes

**Cooking Time:** 50 minutes (20+30 minutes)

**Servings:** 1 loaf

**Difficulty: Easy**

**Ingredients:**

- 2 cups rice flour Potato starch

- 1⁄2 cup Tapioca flour

- 1⁄2 cup Xanthan gum

- 2 1⁄2 teaspoons 2⁄3 cup powdered milk or 1/2 non diary substitute

- 1 1⁄2 teaspoons Salt

- 1 1⁄2 teaspoons egg substitute (optional)

- 3 tablespoons Sugar

- 1 2⁄3 cups lukewarm water

- 1 1⁄2 tablespoons Dry yeast, granules

- tablespoons Butter, melted or margarine

- 1 teaspoon Vinegar

- 3 eggs, room temperature

## Directions:

1. Add yeast to the bread pan.

2. Add all the flours, xanthan/ gum, milk powder, salt, and sugar.

3. Beat the eggs, and mix with water, butter, and vinegar.

4. Choose white bread setting at medium or use 3-4 hour setting.

## Nutrition:

Calories: 126 Cal

Fat      : 2 g

Carbohydrates: 29 g

Protein : 3 g

## 3. All-Purpose White Bread

**Preparation Time:** 2 hours 10 minutes

**Cooking Time:** 40 minutes

**Servings:** 1 loaf

**Difficulty:  Easy**

## Ingredients:

- ¾ cup water at 80 degrees F

- 1 tablespoon melted butter, cooled

- 1 tablespoon sugar

- ¾ teaspoon salt

- 2 tablespoons skim milk powder

- 2 cups white bread flour

- ¾ teaspoon instant yeast

**Directions:**

1 Add all of the ingredients to your bread machine, carefully following the instructions of the manufacturer.

2 Set the program of your bread machine to Basic/White Bread and set crust type to Medium.

3 Press START.

4 Wait until the cycle completes.

5 Once the loaf is ready, take the bucket out and let the loaf cool for 5 minutes.

6 Gently shake the bucket to remove the loaf.

Put to a cooling rack, slice, and serve.

**Nutrition:**

Calories: 140 Cal

Fat     : 2 g

Carbohydrates: 27 g

Protein : 44 g

Fiber: 2 g

## 4. Mustard-Flavored General Bread

**Preparation Time:** 2 hours 10 minutes

**Cooking Time:** 40 minutes

**Servings:** 2 loaves

**Difficulty:  Easy**

**Ingredients:**

- 1¼ cups milk

- 3 tablespoons sunflower milk

- 3 tablespoons sour cream

- 2 tablespoons dry mustard

- 1 whole egg, beaten

- ½ sachet sugar vanilla

- cups flour

- 1 teaspoon dry yeast

- 2 tablespoons sugar

- 2 teaspoon salt

**Directions:**

1   Take out the bread maker's bucket and pour in milk and sunflower oil; stir and then add sour cream and beaten egg.

2   Add flour, salt, sugar, mustard powder, vanilla sugar, and mix well.

3   Make a small groove in the flour and sprinkle the yeast.

4   Transfer the bucket to your bread maker and cover.

5   Set the program of your bread machine to Basic/White Bread and set crust type to Medium.

6   Press START.

7   Wait until the cycle completes.

8   Once the loaf is ready, take the bucket out and let the loaf cool for 5 minutes.

9   Gently shake the bucket to remove the loaf.

10  Transfer to a cooling rack, slice, and serve.

**Nutrition:**

Calories: 340 Cal

Fat      : 10 g

Carbohydrates: 54 g

Protein : 10 g

Fiber: 1 g

Fiber: 1 g

## 5. Country White Bread

**Preparation Time:** 3 hours

**Cooking Time:** 45 minutes

**Servings:** 2 loaves

**Difficulty:  Easy**

**Ingredients:**

- 2 teaspoon active dry yeast

- 1 1/2 tablespoon sugar

- cups bread flour

- 1 1/2 teaspoon salt

- 1 large egg

- 1 1/2 tablespoon butter

- 1 cup warm milk, with a temperature of 110 to 115 degrees F (43 to 46 degrees C)

**Directions:**

1   Put all the liquid ingredients in the pan. Add all the dry ingredients, except the yeast. Use your hand to form a hole in the middle of the dry ingredients. Put the yeast in the hole.

2   Secure the pan in the chamber and close the lid. Choose the basic setting and your preferred crust color. Press starts.

3   Once done, transfer the baked bread to a wire rack. Slice once cooled.

**Nutrition:**

Calories: 105 calories;

Total Carbohydrate: 0 g

Total Fat: 0 g

Protein: 0 g

## 6.  Oatmeal Bread

**Preparation Time:** 3 hours

**Cooking Time:** 45 minutes

**Servings:** 2 loaves

**Difficulty:  Easy**

**Ingredients:**

- teaspoon bread machine yeast

- teaspoon vital wheat gluten

- cups bread flour

- 1 teaspoon salt

- 1 cup instant or regular oatmeal

- tablespoon maple syrup

- 2 tablespoon unsalted butter, cubed

- 1/3 cup water, with a temperature of 80 to 90 degrees F (26 to 32 degrees C)

- 1 1/2 cups buttermilk, with a temperature of 80 to 90 degrees F (26 to 32 degrees C)

**Directions:**

1   Put the ingredients in the pan in this order: buttermilk, water, butter, maple syrup, oatmeal, salt, flour, gluten, and yeast.

2   Secure the pan in the machine, close the lid and turn it on.

3   Choose the basic setting and your preferred crust color and press start.

4   Transfer the baked bread to a wire rack and allow to cool before slicing.

**Nutrition:**

Calories: 269 calories;

Total Carbohydrate: 49 g

Total Fat: 4 g

Protein: 8 g

## 7. Anadama Bread

**Preparation Time:** 3 hours

**Cooking Time:** 45 minutes

**Servings:** 2 loaves

**Difficulty:  Easy**

**Ingredients:**

- 1/2 cup sunflower seeds

- 2 teaspoon bread machine yeast

- 1/2 cups bread flour

- 3/4 cup yellow cornmeal

- 2 tablespoon unsalted butter, cubed

- 1 1/2 teaspoon salt

- 1/4 cup dry skim milk powder

- 1/4 cup molasses

- 1 1/2 cups water, with a temperature of 80 to 90 degrees F (26 to 32 degrees C)

## Directions:

- Put all the ingredients in the pan, except the sunflower seeds, in this order: water, molasses, milk, salt, butter, cornmeal, flour, and yeast.

- Place the pan in the machine and close the lid.

- Put the sunflower seeds in the fruit and nut dispenser.

- Turn the machine on and choose the basic setting and your desired color of the crust. Press starts.

## Nutrition:

Calories: 130 calories;

Total Carbohydrate: 25 g

Total Fat: 2 g

Protein: 3 g

## 8. Apricot Oat

**Preparation Time:** 1 hour 25 minutes

**Cooking Time:** 25 minutes

**Servings:** 1 loaf

**Difficulty: Easy**

**Ingredients:**

- 1/4 cups bread flour

- 2/3 cup rolled oats

- 1 tablespoon white sugar

- 2 teaspoons active dry yeast

- 1 1/2 teaspoons salt

- 1 teaspoon ground cinnamon

- 2 tablespoons butter, cut up

- 1 2/3 cups orange juice

- 1/2 cup diced dried apricots

- 2 tablespoons honey, warmed

**Directions:**

1. Into the pan of bread machine, put the bread ingredients in the order suggested by manufacturer. Then pout in dried apricots before the knead cycle completes.

2. Immediately remove bread from machine when it's done and then glaze with warmed honey. Let to cool completely prior to serving.

**Nutrition:**

Calories: 80 calories;

Total Carbohydrate: 14.4 g

Cholesterol: 5 mg

Total Fat: 2.3 g

Protein: 1.3 g

Sodium: 306 mg

## 9. Buttermilk White Bread

**Preparation Time:** 2 hour 50 minutes

**Cooking Time:** 25 minutes

**Servings:** 1 loaf

**Difficulty:  Easy**

**Ingredients:**

- 1 1/8 cups water

- teaspoon honey

- 1 tablespoon margarine

- 1 1/2 teaspoon salt

- cups bread flour

- 2 teaspoon active dry yeast

- teaspoon powdered buttermilk

**Directions:**

1   Into the pan of bread machine, place the ingredients in the order suggested by the manufacturer.

2   Select medium crust and white bread settings. You can use less yeast during the hot and humid months on summer.

**Nutrition:**

Calories: 34 calories;

Total Carbohydrate: 5.7 g

Cholesterol: 1 mg

Total Fat: 1 g

Protein: 1 g

Sodium: 313 mg

## 10. English muffin Bread

**Preparation Time:** 2 hours 30 minutes

**Cooking Time:** 15 minutes

**Servings:** 2 loaves

**Difficulty:  Easy**

**Ingredients:**

- cups all-purpose flour

- 1/4 teaspoons active dry yeast

- 1/2 tablespoon white sugar

- 1 teaspoon salt

- 1/8 teaspoon baking powder

- 1 cup warm milk

- 1/4 cup water

**Directions:**

1   Into the bread machine pan, put the ingredients according to the manufacturer's recommendations. Set the machine to the dough cycle.

2   Separate the dough into 2 unequal portions and then form into loaves. Put one portion in a 9 x 5 inch loaf pan and the other in a 7 x 3 inch loaf pan it's recommended to use non-

stick pans although greased and floured normal pans will be enough. Cover the pans and let the dough to rise until doubled in size.

3   Bake for about 15 minutes at 205 degrees C (400 degrees F). My grandmother usually bakes for longer to have a more browned and chewier crust.

**Nutrition:**

Calories: 64 calories;

Total Carbohydrate: 12.8 g

Cholesterol: < 1 mg

Total Fat: 0.4 g

Protein: 2.1 g

Sodium: 104 mg

## 11. Homemade Wonderful Bread

**Preparation Time:** 3 hours 25 minutes

**Cooking Time:** 15 minutes

**Servings:** 2 loaves

**Difficulty:  Easy**

**Ingredients:**

- 1/2 teaspoons active dry yeast

- 1/4 cup warm water (110 degrees F/45 degrees C)

- 1 tablespoon white sugar

- cups all-purpose flour

- 1/4 cup dry potato flakes

- 1/4 cup dry milk powder

- teaspoons salt

- 1/4 cup white sugar

- 2 tablespoons margarine

- 1 cup warm water (110 degrees F/45 degrees C)

**Directions:**

1  Prepare the yeast, 1/4 cup warm water and sugar to whisk and then let it sit in 15 minutes.

2  Take all ingredients together with yeast mixture to put in the pan of bread machine according to the recommended order of manufacture. Choose basic and light crust setting.

**Nutrition:**

Calories: 162 calories;

Total Carbohydrate: 31.6 g

Cholesterol: < 1 mg

Total Fat: 1.8 g

Protein: 4.5 g

Sodium: 339 mg

## 12. Honey White Bread

**Preparation Time:** 3 hours 25 minutes

**Cooking Time:** 15 minutes

**Servings:** 1 loaf

**Difficulty:  Easy**

**Ingredients:**

- 1 cup milk

- tablespoons unsalted butter, melted

- tablespoons honey

- cups bread flour

- 3/4 teaspoon salt

- 3/4 teaspoon vitamin c powder

- 3/4 teaspoon ground ginger

- 1 1/2 teaspoons active dry yeast

## Directions:

1 Follow the order as directed in your bread machine manual on how to assemble the ingredients.

2 Use the setting for Basic Bread cycle.

## Nutrition:

Calories: 172 calories;

Total Carbohydrate: 28.9 g

Cholesterol: 9 mg

Total Fat: 3.9 g

Protein: 5 g

Sodium: 155 mg

## 13. Italian Bread

**Preparation Time:** 2 hours 40 minutes

**Cooking Time:** 25- 30 minutes

**Servings:** 1 loaf

**Difficulty: intermediate**

**Ingredients:**

- cups unbleached all-purpose flour

- 1 tablespoon brown sugar

- 1 1/2 teaspoons salt

- 1 1/8 cups warm water (110 degrees F/45 degrees C)

- 1 1/2 tablespoons olive oil

- 1 1/2 teaspoons active dry yeast

- 1 egg

- 1 tablespoon water

- 1 tablespoon sesame seeds

- 1 tablespoon cornmeal

**Directions:**

1  Into the pan of bread machine, add all ingredients apart from cornmeal, sesame seeds, egg, and one tablespoon of water in the order endorsed by machine's manufacturer. Set the machine to the dough cycle.

2  Separate the dough into two parts and shape into loaves. Drizzle cornmeal onto a greased baking sheet. Transfer the loaves onto the pan with the seam side down. Use water to rub the top of the loaves. Allow to rise for about 50 minutes until double.

3  Preheat the oven to 190 degrees C (375 degrees F).

4  Use egg wash to rub the loaves.

5   Put a pan containing hot water at the bottom of oven.

6  You will definitely have very crusty bread and you will be surprised by how much better it will be when you heat in the final five minutes.

**Nutrition:**

Calories: 147 calories;

Total Carbohydrate: 25.9 g

Cholesterol: 16 mg

Total Fat: 2.8 g

Protein: 4.1 g

Sodium: 298 mg

# Chapter 6.   Cheese Bread

## 14. Cream Cheese Bread

**Preparation Time:** 60 minutes

**Cooking Time:** 35 minutes

**Servings:** 1 loaf

**Difficulty:** Intermediate

**Ingredients:**

- 1/2 cup Water

- 1/2 cup Cream cheese, softened

- tablespoons Melted butter

- 1 Beaten egg

- tablespoons Sugar

- 1 teaspoon Salt

- cups Bread flour

- 1 1/2 teaspoons Active dry yeast

**Directions:**

1  Place the ingredients in the pan in the order as suggested by your bread machine

2  Manufacturer.

3  Process on dough cycle.

4  Remove from machine, form into a loaf and place in greased 9x5 loaf pan.

5  Cover and let rise until doubled.

6  Bake in a 350° oven for approximately 35 minutes.

**Nutrition:**

Calories: 150 calories;

Total Carbohydrate: 24 g

Total Fat: 5 g

Protein: 3 g

## 15. Mozzarella Cheese and Salami Loaf

**Preparation Time:** 2 hours 50 minutes

**Cooking Time:** 45 minutes

**Servings:** 1 loaf

**Difficulty:** Intermediate

**Ingredients:**

- ¾ cup water, at 80 degrees F
- 1/3 cup mozzarella cheese, shredded
- teaspoons sugar
- 2/3 teaspoon salt
- 2/3 teaspoon dried basil
- Pinch of garlic powder
- cups + 2 tablespoons white bread flour
- 1 teaspoon instant yeast
- ½ cup hot salami, finely diced

**Directions:**

1. Add the listed ingredients to your bread machine (except salami), following the manufactures instructions.

2. Set the bread machine's program to Basic/White Bread and the crust type to Light. Press Start.

3. Let the bread machine work and wait until it beeps, this your indication to add the remaining ingredients. At this point add the salami.

4. Wait until the remaining bake cycle completes.

5. Once the loaf is done, take the bucket out from the bread machine and let it rest for 5 minutes.

6. Gently shake the bucket and remove the loaf, transfer the loaf to a cooling rack and slice.

7. Serve and enjoy!

**Nutrition:**

Calories: 164 calories;

Total Carbohydrate: 28 g

Total Fat: 3 g

Protein: 6 g

Sugar: 2 g

## 16. Olive and Cheddar Loaf

**Preparation Time:** 2 hours 50 minutes

**Cooking Time:** 45 minutes

**Servings:** 1 loaf

**Difficulty:** Intermediate

**Ingredients:**

- 1 cup water, room temperature

- teaspoons sugar

- ¾ teaspoon salt

- 1 and 1/ cups sharp cheddar cheese, shredded

- cups bread flour

- teaspoons active dry yeast

- ¾ cup pimiento olives, drained and sliced

## Directions:

1  Add the listed ingredients to your bread machine (except salami), following the manufactures instructions.

2  Set the bread machine's program to Basic/White Bread and the crust type to Light. Press Start.

3  Let the bread machine work and wait until it beeps, this your indication to add the remaining ingredients. At this point add the salami.

4  Wait until the remaining bake cycle completes.

5  Once the loaf is done, take the bucket out from the bread machine and let it rest for 5 minutes.

6  Gently shake the bucket and remove the loaf, transfer the loaf to a cooling rack and slice.

7  Serve and enjoy!

## Nutrition:

Calories: 124 calories;

Total Carbohydrate: 19 g

Total Fat: 4 g

Protein: 5 g

Sugar: 5 g

## 17. Cottage Cheese Bread

**Preparation Time:** 2 hours 50 minutes

**Cooking Time:** 45 minutes

**Servings:** 1 loaf

**Difficulty:** Intermediate

**Ingredients:**

- 1/2 cup water

- 1 cup cottage cheese

- tablespoons margarine

- 1 egg

- 1 tablespoon white sugar

- 1/4 teaspoon baking soda

- 1 teaspoon salt

- cups bread flour

- 1/2 teaspoons active dry yeast

**Directions:**

1   Into the bread machine, place the ingredients according to the order recommended by manufacturer and then push the start button.

2   In case the dough looks too sticky, feel free to use up to half cup more bread flour.

**Nutrition:**

Calories: 171 calories;

Total Carbohydrate: 26.8 g

Cholesterol: 18 mg

Total Fat: 3.6 g

Protein: 7.3 g

Sodium: 324 mg

## 18. Green Cheese Bread

**Preparation Time:** 3 hours

**Cooking Time:** 15 minutes

**Servings:** 8

**Difficulty:** Intermediate

**Ingredients:**

- ¾ cup lukewarm water

- 1 Tablespoon sugar

- 1 teaspoon kosher salt

- Tablespoon green cheese

- 1 cup wheat bread machine flour

- 9/10 cup whole-grain flour, finely ground

- 1 teaspoon bread machine yeast

- 1 teaspoon ground paprika

**Directions:**

1   Place all the dry and liquid ingredients, except paprika, in the pan and follow the instructions for your bread machine.

2   Pay particular attention to measuring the ingredients. Use a measuring cup, measuring spoon, and kitchen scales to do so.

3   Dissolve yeast in warm milk in a saucepan and add in the last turn.

4   Add paprika after the beep or place it in the dispenser of the bread machine.

5   Set the baking program to BASIC and the crust type to DARK.

6   If the dough is too dense or too wet, adjust the amount of flour and liquid in the recipe.

7   When the program has ended, take the pan out of the bread machine and let cool for 5 minutes.

8   Shake the loaf out of the pan. If necessary, use a spatula.

9   Wrap the bread with a kitchen towel and set it aside for an hour. Otherwise, you can cool it on a wire rack.

**Nutrition:**

Calories: 118 calories;

Total Carbohydrate: 23.6 g

Cholesterol: 2 g

Total Fat: 1 g

Protein: 4.1 g

Sodium: 304 mg

Sugar: 1.6 g

Fiber: 1 g

## 19. Cheesy Chipotle Bread

**Preparation Time:** 2 hours

**Cooking Time:** 15 minutes

**Servings:** 8

**Difficulty:** Intermediate

**Ingredients:**

- ⅔ cup water, at 80°F to 90°F
- 1½ tablespoons sugar
- 1½ tablespoons powdered skim milk
- ¾ teaspoon salt
- ½ teaspoon chipotle chili powder
- cups white bread flour
- ½ cup (2 ounces) shredded sharp Cheddar cheese
- ¾ teaspoon bread machine or instant yeast

- **Directions:**

1  Place the ingredients in your bread machine as recommended by the manufacturer.

2  Program the machine for Basic/White bread, select light or medium crust, and press Start.

3  When the loaf is done, remove the bucket from the machine.

4  Let the loaf cool for 5 minutes.

5  Gently shake the bucket to remove the loaf, and turn it out onto a rack to cool.

**Nutrition:**

Calories: 139 calories;

Total Carbohydrate: 27 g

Total Fat: 1g

Protein: 6 g

Sodium: 245 mg

Fiber: 1 g

## 20. Cheddar Cheese Basil Bread

**Preparation Time:** 2 hours

**Cooking Time:** 15 minutes

**Servings:** 8

**Ingredients:**

- ⅔ cup milk, at 80°F to 90°F

- teaspoons melted butter, cooled

- teaspoons sugar

- ⅔ Teaspoon dried basil

- ½ cup (2 ounces) shredded sharp Cheddar cheese

- ½ teaspoon salt

- cups white bread flour

- 1 teaspoon bread machine or active dry yeast

**Directions:**

1   Place the ingredients in your bread machine as recommended by the manufacturer.

2   Program the machine for Basic/White bread, select light or medium crust, and press Start.

3   When the loaf is done, remove the bucket from the machine.

4   Let the loaf cool for 5 minutes.

5   Gently shake the bucket to remove the loaf, and turn it out onto a rack to cool.

**Nutrition:**

Calories: 166 calories;

Total Carbohydrate: 26 g

Total Fat: 4g

Protein: 6 g

Sodium: 209 mg

Fiber: 1 g

## 21. Olive Cheese Bread

**Preparation Time:** 2 hours

**Cooking Time:** 15 minutes

**Servings:** 8

**Difficulty:** Intermediate

**Ingredients:**

- ⅔ Cup milk, at 80°F to 90°F
- 1 tablespoon melted butter, cooled
- ⅔ Teaspoon minced garlic
- 1 tablespoon sugar
- ⅔ Teaspoon salt
- cups white bread flour
- ½ cup (2 ounces) shredded Swiss cheese
- ¾ teaspoon bread machine or instant yeast
- ¼ cup chopped black olives

**Directions:**

1    Place the ingredients in your bread machine as recommended by the manufacturer.

2 Program the machine for Basic/White bread, select light or medium crust, and press Start.

3 When the loaf is done, remove the bucket from the machine.

4 Let the loaf cool for 5 minutes.

5 Gently shake the bucket to remove the loaf, and turn it out onto a rack to cool.

**Nutrition:**

Calories: 175 calories;

Total Carbohydrate: 27 g

Total Fat: 5g

Protein: 6 g

Sodium: 260 mg

Fiber: 1 g

## 22. Double Cheese Bread

**Preparation Time:** 2 hours

**Cooking Time:** 15 minutes

**Servings:** 8

**Difficulty:** Intermediate

**Ingredients:**

- ¾ cup plus 1 tablespoon milk, at 80°F to 90°F
- teaspoons butter, melted and cooled
- teaspoons sugar
- ⅔ teaspoon salt
- ⅓ teaspoon freshly ground black pepper

- Pinch cayenne pepper

- 1 cup (4 ounces) shredded aged sharp Cheddar cheese

- ⅓ cup shredded or grated Parmesan cheese

- cups white bread flour

- ¾ teaspoon bread machine or instant yeast

## Directions:

1  Place the ingredients in your bread machine as recommended by the manufacturer.

2  Program the machine for Basic/White bread, select light or medium crust, and press Start.

3  When the loaf is done, remove the bucket from the machine.

4  Let the loaf cool for 5 minutes.

5  Gently shake the bucket to remove the loaf, and turn it out onto a rack to cool.

## Nutrition:

Calories: 183 calories;

Total Carbohydrate: 28 g

Total Fat: 4g

Protein: 6 g

Sodium: 344 mg

Fiber: 1 g

## 23. Chile Cheese Bacon Bread

**Preparation Time:** 2 hours

**Cooking Time:** 15 minutes

**Servings:** 8

**Difficulty:** Intermediate

**Ingredients:**

- ⅓ Cup milk, at 80°F to 90°F

- 1 teaspoon melted butter, cooled

- 1 tablespoon honey

- 1 teaspoon salt

- ⅓ Cup chopped and drained green Chile

- ⅓ Cup grated Cheddar cheese

- ⅓ cup chopped cooked bacon

- cups white bread flour

- 1⅓ teaspoons bread machine or instant yeast

**Directions:**

1   Place the ingredients in your bread machine as recommended by the manufacturer.

2   Program the machine for Basic/White bread, select light or medium crust, and press Start.

3   When the loaf is done, remove the bucket from the machine.

4   Let the loaf cool for 5 minutes.

5   Gently shake the bucket to remove the loaf, and turn it out onto a rack to cool.

**Nutrition:**

Calories: 174 calories;

Total Carbohydrate: 404 g

Total Fat: 4 g

Protein: 6 g

Sodium: 1 mg

Fiber: 1 g

## 24. Italian Parmesan Bread

**Preparation Time:** 2 hours

**Cooking Time:** 15 minutes

**Servings:** 8

**Difficulty:** Intermediate

**Ingredients:**

- ¾ cup water, at 80°F to 90°F

- tablespoons melted butter, cooled

- teaspoons sugar

- ⅔ teaspoon salt

- 1⅓ teaspoons chopped fresh basil

- 2⅔ tablespoons grated Parmesan cheese

- 2⅓ cups white bread flour

- 1 teaspoon bread machine or instant yeast

**Directions:**

1  Place the ingredients in your bread machine as recommended by the manufacturer.

2  Program the machine for Basic/White bread, select light or medium crust, and press Start.

3  When the loaf is done, remove the bucket from the machine.

4  Gently shake the bucket to remove the loaf, and turn it out onto a rack to cool.

**Nutrition:**

Calories: 171 calories;

Total Carbohydrate: 29 g

Total Fat: 4 g

Protein: 5 g

Sodium: 237 mg

Fiber: 1 g

## 25. Feta Oregano Bread

**Preparation Time:** 2 hours

**Cooking Time:** 15 minutes

**Servings:** 8

**Ingredients:**

- ⅔ Cup milk, at 80°F to 90°F

- teaspoons melted butter, cooled

- teaspoons sugar

- ⅔ Teaspoon salt

- teaspoons dried oregano

- cups white bread flour

- 1½ teaspoons bread machine or instant yeast

- ⅔ cup (2½ ounces) crumbled feta cheese

**Directions:**

1  Place the ingredients in your bread machine as recommended by the manufacturer.

2  Program the machine for Basic/White bread, select light or medium crust, and press Start.

3  When the loaf is done, remove the bucket from the machine.

4    Let the loaf cool for 5 minutes.

5    Gently shake the bucket to remove the loaf, and turn it out onto a rack to cool.

**Nutrition:**

Calories: 164 calories;

Total Carbohydrate: 27 g

Total Fat: 4 g

Protein: 5 g

Sodium: 316 mg

Fiber: 2 g

## 26. French Cheese Bread

**Preparation Time:** 5 minutes

**Cooking Time:** 3 hours and 45 minutes

**Servings:** 14 slices

**Difficulty:** Intermediate

**Ingredients:**

- 1 teaspoon sugar

- 2¼ teaspoon yeast

- 1¼ cup water

- 3 cups bread flour

- 2 Tablespoon parmesan cheese

- 1 teaspoon garlic powder

- 1½ teaspoon salt

## Directions

1.  Add each ingredient to the bread machine in the order and at the temperature recommended by your bread machine manufacturer.

2.  Close the lid, select the basic bread, medium crust setting on your bread machine, and press start.

3.  When the bread machine has finished baking, remove the bread and put it on a cooling rack.

Nutrition:

Carbs: 21 g

Fat: 6 g

Protein: 8 g

Calories: 170

## 27. Beer Cheese Bread

**Preparation Time:** 10 minutes

**Cooking Time:** 2 hours and 10 minutes

**Servings:** 14 slices

**Difficulty:** Expert

**Ingredients:**

- 1 package active dry yeast

- 3 cups bread flour

- 1 Tablespoon sugar

- 1½ teaspoon salt

- 1 Tablespoon room temperature butter

- 1¼ cup room temperature beer

- ½ cup shredded or diced American cheese

- ½ cup shredded or diced Monterey jack cheese

**Directions:**

1. Heat the beer and American cheese in the microwave together until just warm.

2. Add each ingredient to the bread machine in the order and at the temperature recommended by your bread machine manufacturer.

3. Close the lid, select the basic bread, medium crust setting on your bread machine and press start.

4. When the bread machine has finished baking, remove the bread and put it on a cooling rack.

Nutrition:

Carbs: 21 g

Fat: 5 g

Protein: 5 g

Calories: 144

## 28.Jalapeno Cheese Bread

**Preparation Time:** 5 minutes

**Cooking Time:** 3 hours

**Servings:** 14 slices

**Difficulty:** Intermediate

**Ingredients:**

- 3 cups bread flour

- 1½ teaspoon active dry yeast

- 1 cup water

- 2 Tablespoon sugar

- 1 teaspoon salt

- ½ cup shredded cheddar cheese

- ¼ cup diced jalapeno peppers

**Directions:**

1. Add each ingredient to the bread machine in the order and at the temperature recommended by your bread machine manufacturer.

2. Close the lid, select the basic bread, medium crust setting on your bread machine, and press start.

3. When the bread machine has finished baking, remove the bread and put it on a cooling rack.

Nutrition:

Carbs: 22 g

Fat: 4 g

Protein: 7 g

Calories: 150

## 29. Cheddar Cheese Bread

**Preparation Time:** 5 minutes

**Cooking Time:** 3 hours and 10 minutes

**Servings:** 14 slices

**Difficulty:** Intermediate

**Ingredients:**

- 1 cup lukewarm milk

- 3 cups all-purpose flour

- 1¼ teaspoon salt

- 1 teaspoon tabasco sauce, optional

- ¼ cup Vermont cheese powder

- 1 Tablespoon sugar

- 1 cup grated cheddar cheese, firmly packed

- 1 1/2 teaspoon instant yeast

**Directions:**

1. Add each ingredient to the bread machine in the order and at the temperature recommended by your bread machine manufacturer.

2. Close the lid, select the basic bread, medium crust setting on your bread machine, and press start.

3. When the bread machine has finished baking, remove the bread and put it on a cooling rack.

Nutrition:

Carbs: 25 g

Fat: 4 g

Protein: 7 g

Calories: 165

# 30. Cottage Cheese and Chive Bread

**Preparation Time:** 10 minutes

**Cooking Time:** 3 hours

**Servings:** 14 slices

**Difficulty:** Intermediate

**Ingredients:**

- 3/8 cup water

- 1 cup cottage cheese

- 1 large egg

- 2 Tablespoon butter

- 1½ teaspoon salt

- 3¾ cups white bread flour

- 3 Tablespoon dried chives

- 2½ Tablespoon granulated sugar

- 2¼ teaspoon active dry yeast

## Directions:

1. Add each ingredient to the bread machine in the order and at the temperature recommended by your bread machine manufacturer.

2. Close the lid, select the basic bread, medium crust setting on your bread machine, and press start.

3. When the bread machine has finished baking, remove the bread and put it on a cooling rack.

Nutrition:

Carbs: 33 g

Fat: 4 g

Protein: 7 g

Calories: 196

## 31. Ricotta Bread

**Preparation Time:** 5 minutes

**Cooking Time:** 3 hours and 15 minutes

**Servings:** 14 slices

**Difficulty:** Intermediate

**Ingredients:**

- 3 Tablespoon skim milk

- 2/3 cup ricotta cheese

- 4 teaspoon unsalted butter, softened to room temperature

- 1 large egg

- 2 Tablespoon granulated sugar

- ½ teaspoon salt

- 1½ cups bread flour, + more flour, as needed

- 1 teaspoon active dry yeast

**Directions:**

1. Add each ingredient to the bread machine in the order and at the temperature recommended by your bread machine manufacturer.

2. Close the lid, select the basic bread, medium crust setting on your bread machine, and press start.

3. When the bread machine has finished baking, remove the bread and put it on a cooling rack.

Nutrition:

Carbs: 3 g

Fat: 12 g

Protein: 11 g

Calories: 174

## 32. Oregano Cheese Bread

**Preparation Time:** 10 minutes

**Cooking Time:** 2 hours and 5 minutes

**Servings:** 14 slices

**Difficulty:** Intermediate

**Ingredients:**

- 3 cups bread flour

- 1 cup water

- ½ cup freshly grated parmesan cheese

- 3 Tablespoon sugar

- 1 Tablespoon dried leaf oregano

- 1½ Tablespoon olive oil

- 1 teaspoon salt

- 2 teaspoon active dry yeast

**Directions:**

1. Add each ingredient to the bread machine in the order and at the temperature recommended by your bread machine manufacturer.

2. Close the lid, select the basic bread, medium crust setting on your bread machine, and press start.

3. When the bread machine has finished baking, remove the bread and put it on a cooling rack.

Nutrition:

Carbs: 22 g

Fat: 5 g

Protein: 3 g

Calories: 146

## 33. Spinach and Feta Bread

**Preparation Time:** 10 minutes

**Cooking Time:** 4 hours and 15 minutes

**Servings:** 14 slices

**Difficulty:** Intermediate

**Ingredients:**

- 1 cup water

- 2 teaspoon butter

- 3 cups flour

- 1 teaspoon sugar

- 2 teaspoon instant minced onion

- 1 teaspoon salt

- 1¼ teaspoon instant yeast

- 1 cup crumbled feta

- 1 cup chopped fresh spinach leaves

**Directions:**

1. Add each ingredient except the cheese and spinach to the bread machine in the order and at the temperature recommended by your bread machine manufacturer.

2. Close the lid, select the basic bread, medium crust setting on your bread machine, and press start.

3. When only 10 minutes are left in the last kneading cycle add the spinach and cheese.

4. When the bread machine has finished baking, remove the bread and put it on a cooling rack.

Nutrition:

Carbs: 16 g

Fat: 6 g

Protein: 6 g

Calories: 140

## 34. Italian Cheese Bread

**Preparation Time:** 10 minutes

**Cooking Time:** 2 hours

**Servings:** 14 slices

**Difficulty:** Intermediate

**Ingredients:**

- 1¼ cups water

- 3 cups bread flour

- ½ shredded pepper jack cheese

- 2 teaspoon Italian seasoning

- 2 Tablespoon brown sugar

- 1½ teaspoon salt

- 2 teaspoon active dry yeast

**Directions:**

1. Add each ingredient to the bread machine in the order and at the temperature recommended by your bread machine manufacturer.

2. Close the lid, select the basic bread, medium crust setting on your bread machine, and press start.

3. When the bread machine has finished baking, remove the bread and put it on a cooling rack.

Nutrition:

Carbs: 13 g

Fat: 6 g

Protein: 7 g

Calories: 130

## 35. Onion, Garlic, Cheese Bread

**Preparation Time:** 50 minutes

**Cooking Time:** 40 minutes

**Servings:** 1 loaf

**Difficulty:** Intermediate

**Ingredients:**

- tablespoon Dried minced onion

- cups bread flour

- teaspoon Garlic powder

- teaspoon Active dry yeast

- tablespoon White sugar

- 2 tablespoon Margarine

- 2 tablespoon Dry milk powder

- 1 cup shredded sharp cheddar cheese

- 1 1/8 cups warm water

- 1 1/2 teaspoon Salt

## Directions:

1   In the order suggested by the manufacturer, put the flour, water, powdered milk, margarine or butter, salt, and yeast in the bread pan.

2   Press the basic cycle with light crust. When the sound alerts or as directed by the manufacturer, add 2 teaspoon of the onion flakes, the garlic powder, and all of the shredded cheese.

3   After the last kneed, sprinkle the remaining onion flakes over the dough.

## Nutrition:

Calories: 204 calories;

Total Carbohydrate: 29 g

Total Fat: 6 g

Protein: 8 g

# Chapter 7. Vegetable Breads

## 36. Healthy Celery Loaf

**Preparation Time:** 2 hours 40 minutes

**Cooking Time:** 50 minutes

**Servings:** 1 loaf

**Difficulty:** Expert

**Ingredients:**

- 1 can (10 ounces) cream of celery soup

- tablespoons low-fat milk, heated

- 1 tablespoon vegetable oil

- 1¼ teaspoons celery salt

- ¾ cup celery, fresh/sliced thin

- 1 tablespoon celery leaves, fresh, chopped

- 1 whole egg

- ¼ teaspoon sugar

- cups bread flour

- ¼ teaspoon ginger

- ½ cup quick-cooking oats

- tablespoons gluten

- teaspoons celery seeds

1 pack of active dry yeast

**Directions:**

1. Add all of the ingredients to your bread machine, carefully following the instructions of the manufacturer

2. Set the program of your bread machine to Basic/White Bread and set crust type to Medium

3. Press START

4. Wait until the cycle completes

5. Once the loaf is ready, take the bucket out and let the loaf cool for 5 minutes

6. Gently shake the bucket to remove the loaf

7. Transfer to a cooling rack, slice and serve

8. Enjoy!

**Nutrition:**

Calories: 73 Cal

Fat: 4 g

Carbohydrates:8 g

Protein: 3 g

Fiber: 1 g

## 37. Broccoli and Cauliflower Bread

**Preparation Time:** 2 hours 20 minutes

**Cooking Time:** 50 minutes

**Servings:** 1 loaf

**Difficulty:** Expert

**Ingredients:**

- ¼ cup water

- tablespoons olive oil

- 1 egg white

- 1 teaspoon lemon juice

- 2/3 cup grated cheddar cheese

- tablespoons green onion

- ½ cup broccoli, chopped

- ½ cup cauliflower, chopped

- ½ teaspoon lemon pepper seasoning

- cups bread flour

- 1 teaspoon bread machine yeast

**Directions:**

1. Add all of the ingredients to your bread machine, carefully following the instructions of the manufacturer

2. Set the program of your bread machine to Basic/White Bread and set crust type to Medium

3. Press START

4. Wait until the cycle completes

5. Once the loaf is ready, take the bucket out and let the loaf cool for 5 minutes

6. Gently shake the bucket to remove the loaf

7. Transfer to a cooling rack, slice and serve

8. Enjoy!

**Nutrition:**

Calories: 156 Cal

Fat: 8 g

Carbohydrates:17 g

Protein: 5 g

Fiber: 2 g

## 38. Zucchini Herbed Bread

**Preparation Time:** 2 hours 20 minutes

**Cooking Time:** 50 minutes

**Servings:** 1 loaf

**Difficulty:** Intermediate

**Ingredients:**

- ½ cup water
- teaspoon honey
- 1 tablespoons oil
- ¾ cup zucchini, grated
- ¾ cup whole wheat flour
- cups bread flour
- 1 tablespoon fresh basil, chopped
- teaspoon sesame seeds
- 1 teaspoon salt
- 1½ teaspoon active dry yeast

**Directions:**

1. Add all of the ingredients to your bread machine, carefully following the instructions of the manufacturer

2. Set the program of your bread machine to Basic/White Bread and set crust type to Medium

3. Press START

4. Wait until the cycle completes

5. Once the loaf is ready, take the bucket out and let the loaf cool for 5 minutes

6. Gently shake the bucket to remove the loaf

7. Transfer to a cooling rack, slice and serve

8. Enjoy!

**Nutrition:**

Calories: 153 Cal

Fat: 1 g

Carbohydrates:28 g

Protein: 5 g

Fiber: 2 g

## 39. Potato Bread

**Preparation Time:** 3 hours

**Cooking Time:** 45 minutes

**Servings:** 2 loaves

**Difficulty:** Intermediate

## Ingredients:

- 1 3/4 teaspoon active dry yeast
- tablespoon dry milk
- 1/4 cup instant potato flakes
- tablespoon sugar
- cups bread flour
- 1 1/4 teaspoon salt
- tablespoon butter
- 1 3/8 cups water

## Directions:

1   Put all the liquid ingredients in the pan. Add all the dry ingredients, except the yeast. Form a shallow hole in the middle of the dry ingredients and place the yeast.

2   Secure the pan in the machine and close the lid. Choose the basic setting and your desired color of the crust. Press starts.

3   Allow the bread to cool before slicing.

## Nutrition:

Calories: 35calories;

Total Carbohydrate: 19 g

Total Fat: 0 g

Protein: 4 g

## 40. Golden Potato Bread

**Preparation Time:** 2 hours 50 minutes

**Cooking Time:** 45 minutes

**Servings:** 2 loaves

**Difficulty:** Expert

**Ingredients:**

- teaspoon bread machine yeast

- cups bread flour

- 1 1/2 teaspoon salt

- tablespoon potato starch

- 1 tablespoon dried chives

- tablespoon dry skim milk powder

- 1 teaspoon sugar

- tablespoon unsalted butter, cubed

- 3/4 cup mashed potatoes

- 1 large egg, at room temperature

- 3/4 cup potato cooking water, with a temperature of 80 to 90 degrees F (26 to 32 degrees C)

**Directions:**

1   Prepare the mashed potatoes. Peel the potatoes and put them in a saucepan. Pour enough cold water to cover them. Turn the heat to high and bring to a boil. Turn the heat to low and continue cooking the potatoes until tender. Transfer the cooked potatoes to a bowl and mash. Cover the bowl until the potatoes are ready to use. Reserve cooking water and cook until it reaches the needed temperature.

2   Put the ingredients in the bread pan in this order: potato cooking water, egg, mashed potatoes, butter, sugar, milk, chives, potato starch, salt, flour, and yeast.

3   Place the pan in the machine and close the lid. Turn it on. Choose the sweet setting and your preferred crust color. Start the cooking process.

4   Gently unmold the baked bread and leave to cool on a wire rack.

5   Slice and serve.

**Nutrition:**

Calories: 90calories;

Total Carbohydrate: 15 g

Total Fat: 2 g

Protein: 4 g

Protein: 4 g

## 41. Onion Potato Bread

**Preparation Time:** 1 hour 20 minutes

**Cooking Time:** 45 minutes

**Servings:** 2 loaves

**Difficulty:** Intermediate

**Ingredients:**

- tablespoon quick rise yeast
- cups bread flour
- 1 1/2 teaspoon seasoned salt
- tablespoon sugar
- 2/3 cup baked potatoes, mashed
- 1 1/2 cup onions, minced

- large eggs

- tablespoon oil

- 3/4 cup hot water, with the temperature of 115 to 125 degrees F (46 to 51 degrees C)

**Directions:**

1   Put the liquid ingredients in the pan. Add the dry ingredients, except the yeast. Form a shallow well in the middle using your hand and put the yeast.

2   Place the pan in the machine, close the lid and turn it on. Select the express bake 80 setting and start the machine.

3   Once the bread is cooked, leave on a wire rack for 20 minutes or until cooled.

**Nutrition:**

Calories: 160calories;

Total Carbohydrate: 44 g

Total Fat: 2 g

Protein: 6 g

## 42. Spinach Bread

**Preparation Time:** 2 hours 20 minutes

**Cooking Time:** 40 minutes

**Servings:** 1 loaf

**Difficulty:** Intermediate

**Ingredients:**

- 1 cup water

- 1 tablespoon vegetable oil

- 1/2 cup frozen chopped spinach, thawed and drained

- cups all-purpose flour

- 1/2 cup shredded Cheddar cheese

- 1 teaspoon salt

- 1 tablespoon white sugar

- 1/2 teaspoon ground black pepper

- 1/2 teaspoons active dry yeast

## Directions:

1  In the pan of bread machine, put all ingredients according to the suggested order of manufacture. Set white bread cycle.

## Nutrition:

Calories: 121 calories;

Total Carbohydrate: 20.5 g

Cholesterol: 4 mg

Total Fat: 2.5 g

Protein: 4 g

Sodium: 184 mg

## 43. Curd Bread

**Preparation Time:** 4 hours

**Cooking Time:** 15 minutes

**Servings:** 12

**Difficulty:** Intermediate

## Ingredients:

- ¾ cup lukewarm water
- 2/3 cups wheat bread machine flour
- ¾ cup cottage cheese
- Tablespoon softened butter
- Tablespoon white sugar
- 1½ teaspoon sea salt
- 1½ Tablespoon sesame seeds
- Tablespoon dried onions
- 1¼ teaspoon bread machine yeast

## Directions:

2  Place all the dry and liquid ingredients in the pan and follow the instructions for your bread machine.

3  Pay particular attention to measuring the ingredients. Use a measuring cup, measuring spoon, and kitchen scales to do so.

4  Set the baking program to BASIC and the crust type to MEDIUM.

5  If the dough is too dense or too wet, adjust the amount of flour and liquid in the recipe.

6  When the program has ended, take the pan out of the bread machine and let cool for 5 minutes.

7  Shake the loaf out of the pan. If necessary, use a spatula.

8  Wrap the bread with a kitchen towel and set it aside for an hour. Otherwise, you can cool it on a wire rack.

## Nutrition:

Calories: 277 calories;

Total Carbohydrate: 48.4 g

Cholesterol: 9 g

Total Fat: 4.7g

Protein: 9.4 g

Sodium: 547 mg

Sugar: 3.3 g

## 44. Curvy Carrot Bread

**Preparation Time:** 2 hours

**Cooking Time:** 15 minutes

**Servings:** 12

**Difficulty:** Intermediate

**Ingredients:**

- ¾ cup milk, lukewarm
- tablespoons butter, melted at room temperature
- 1 tablespoon honey
- ¾ teaspoon ground nutmeg
- ½ teaspoon salt
- 1 ½ cups shredded carrot
- cups white bread flour
- ¼ teaspoons bread machine or active dry yeast

**Directions:**

1   Take 1 ½ pound size loaf pan and first add the liquid ingredients and then add the dry ingredients.

2   Place the loaf pan in the machine and close its top lid.

3   Plug the bread machine into power socket. For selecting a bread cycle, press "Quick Bread/Rapid Bread" and for selecting a crust type, press "Light" or "Medium".

4   Start the machine and it will start preparing the bread.

5   After the bread loaf is completed, open the lid and take out the loaf pan.

6   Allow the pan to cool down for 10-15 minutes on a wire rack. Gently shake the pan and remove the bread loaf.

7   Make slices and serve.

**Nutrition:**

Calories: 142 calories;

Total Carbohydrate: 32.2 g

Cholesterol: 0 g

Total Fat: 0.8 g

Protein: 2.33 g

## 45. Potato Rosemary Bread

**Preparation Time:** 3 hours

**Cooking Time:** 30 minutes

**Servings:** 20

**Difficulty:** Intermediate

**Ingredients:**

- cups bread flour, sifted

- 1 tablespoon white sugar

- 1 tablespoon sunflower oil

- 1½ teaspoons salt

- 1½ cups lukewarm water

- 1 teaspoon active dry yeast

- 1 cup potatoes, mashed

- teaspoons crushed rosemary

## Directions:

1  Prepare all of the ingredients for your bread and measuring means (a cup, a spoon, kitchen scales).

2  Carefully measure the ingredients into the pan, except the potato and rosemary.

3  Place all of the ingredients into the bread bucket in the right order, following the manual for your bread machine.

4  Close the cover.

5  Select the program of your bread machine to BREAD with FILLINGS and choose the crust color to MEDIUM.

6  Press START.

7  After the signal, put the mashed potato and rosemary to the dough.

8  Wait until the program completes.

9  When done, take the bucket out and let it cool for 5-10 minutes.

10 Shake the loaf from the pan and let cool for 30 minutes on a cooling rack.

11 Slice, serve and enjoy the taste of fragrant homemade bread.

## Nutrition:

Calories: 106 calories;

Total Carbohydrate: 21 g

Total Fat: 1 g

Protein: 2.9 g

Sodium: 641 mg

Fiber: 1 g

Sugar: 0.8 g

## 46. Beetroot Prune Bread

**Preparation Time:** 3 hours

**Cooking Time:** 30 minutes

**Servings:** 20

**Difficulty:** Intermediate

**Ingredients**:

- 1½ cups lukewarm beet broth
- 5¼ cups all-purpose flour
- 1 cup beet puree
- 1 cup prunes, chopped
- tablespoons extra virgin olive oil
- tablespoons dry cream
- 1 tablespoon brown sugar
- teaspoons active dry yeast
- 1 tablespoon whole milk

- teaspoons sea salt

## Directions:

1   Prepare all of the ingredients for your bread and measuring means (a cup, a spoon, kitchen scales).

2   Carefully measure the ingredients into the pan, except the prunes.

3   Place all of the ingredients into the bread bucket in the right order, following the manual for your bread machine.

4   Close the cover.

5   Select the program of your bread machine to BASIC and choose the crust color to MEDIUM.

6   Press START.

7   After the signal, put the prunes to the dough.

8   Wait until the program completes.

9   When done, take the bucket out and let it cool for 5-10 minutes.

10  Shake the loaf from the pan and let cool for 30 minutes on a cooling rack.

11  Slice, serve and enjoy the taste of fragrant homemade bread.

## Nutrition:

Calories: 443 calories;

Total Carbohydrate: 81.1 g

Total Fat: 8.2 g

Protein: 9.9 g

Sodium: 604 mg

Fiber: 4.4 g

Sugar: 11.7 g

# Chapter 8.    Spice And Herb Bread

## 47. Original Italian Herb Bread

**Preparation Time:** 15 minutes

**Cooking Time:** 3 hours

**Servings:** 20 slices

**Difficulty:** Intermediate

**Ingredients:**

- 1 cup water at 80 degrees F

- ½ cup olive brine

- 1½ tablespoons butter

- 3 tablespoons sugar

- 2 teaspoons salt

- 5 1/3 cups flour

- 2 teaspoons bread machine yeast

- 20 olives, black/green

- 1½ teaspoons Italian herbs

**Directions:**

1. Cut olives into slices.

2. Put all ingredients to your bread machine (except olives), carefully following the instructions of the manufacturer.

3. Set the program of your bread machine to French bread and set crust type to Medium.

4. Once the maker beeps, add olives.

5. Wait until the cycle completes.

6. Once the loaf is ready, take the bucket out and cool the loaf for 6 minutes.

7. Wobble the bucket to take off the loaf.

Nutrition:

Total Carbs: 71g

Fiber: 1g

Protein: 10g

Fat: 7g

Calories: 386

## 48. Lovely Aromatic Lavender BreadErrore. Il segnalibro non è definito.

**Preparation Time:** 5 minutes

**Cooking Time:** 2 hours and 45 minutes

**Servings:** 8 slices

**Difficulty:** Expert

**Ingredients:**

- ¾ cup milk at 80 degrees F

- 1 tablespoon melted butter, cooled

- 1 tablespoon sugar

- ¾ teaspoon salt

- 1 teaspoon fresh lavender flower, chopped

- ¼ teaspoon lemon zest

- ¼ teaspoon fresh thyme, chopped

- 2 cups white bread flour

- ¾ teaspoon instant yeast

**Directions:**

1. Add all of the ingredients to your bread machine, carefully following the instructions of the manufacturer.

2. Set the program of your bread machine to Basic/White Bread and set crust type to Medium.

3. Wait until the cycle completes.

4. Once the loaf is ready, take the bucket out and let the loaf cool for 5 minutes.

5. Gently shake the bucket to remove the loaf.

Nutrition:

Total Carbs: 27g

Fiber: 1g

Protein: 4g

Fat: 2g

Calories: 144

# 49. Cinnamon & Dried Fruits Bread

**Preparation Time:** 5 minutes

**Cooking Time:** 3 hours

**Servings:** 16 slices

**Difficulty:** Intermediate

**Ingredients:**

- 2¾ cups flour

- 1½ cups dried fruits

- 4 tablespoons sugar

- 2½ tablespoons butter

- 1 tablespoon milk powder

- 1 teaspoon cinnamon

- ½ teaspoon ground nutmeg

- ¼ teaspoon vanillin

- ½ cup peanuts

- powdered sugar, for sprinkling

- 1 teaspoon salt

- 1½ bread machine yeast

## Directions:

1. Add all of the ingredients to your bread machine (except peanuts and powdered sugar), carefully following the instructions of the manufacturer.

2. Set the program of your bread machine to Basic/White Bread and set crust type to Medium.

3. Once the bread maker beeps, moisten dough with a bit of water and add peanuts.

4. Wait until the cycle completes.

5. Once the loaf is ready, take the bucket out and let the loaf cool for 5 minutes.

6. Gently shake the bucket to remove the loaf.

7. Sprinkle with powdered sugar.

Nutrition:

Total Carbs: 65g

Fiber: 1g

Protein: 5g

Fat: 4g

Calories: 315

# 50. Herbal Garlic Cream Cheese Delight

**Preparation Time:** 5 minutes

**Cooking Time:** 2 hours and 45 minutes

**Servings:** 8 slices

**Difficulty:** Intermediate

**Ingredients:**

- 1/3 cup water at 80 degrees F

- 1/3 cup herb and garlic cream cheese mix, at room temp

- 1 whole egg, beaten, at room temp

- 4 teaspoons melted butter, cooled

- 1 tablespoon sugar

- 2/3 teaspoon salt

- 2 cups white bread flour

- 1 teaspoon instant yeast

**Directions:**

1. Add all of the ingredients to your bread machine, carefully following the instructions of the manufacturer.

2. Set the program of your bread machine to Basic/White Bread and set crust type to Medium.

3. Wait until the cycle completes.

4. Once the loaf is ready, take the bucket out and let the loaf cool for 5 minutes.

5. Gently shake the bucket to remove the loaf.

Nutrition:

Total Carbs: 27g

Fiber: 2g

Protein: 5g

Fat: 6g

Calories: 182

# 51. Oregano Mozza-Cheese Bread

**Preparation Time:** 15 minutes

**Cooking Time:** 3 hours and 15 minutes

**Servings:** 16 slices

**Difficulty:** Intermediate

**Ingredients:**

- 1 cup (milk + egg) mixture

- ½ cup mozzarella cheese

- 2¼ cups flour

- ¾ cup whole grain flour

- 2 tablespoons sugar

- 1 teaspoon salt

- 2 teaspoons oregano

- 1½ teaspoons dry yeast

## Directions:

1. Add all of the ingredients to your bread machine, carefully following the instructions of the manufacturer.

2. Set the program of your bread machine to Basic/White Bread and set crust type to Dark.

3. Wait until the cycle completes.

4. Once the loaf is ready, take the bucket out and let the loaf cool for 5 minutes.

5. Gently shake the bucket to remove the loaf.

Nutrition:

Total Carbs: 40g

Fiber: 1g

Protein: 7.7g

Fat: 2.1g

Calories: 209

# 52. Cumin Tossed Fancy Bread

**Preparation Time:** 5 minutes

**Cooking Time:** 3 hours and 15 minutes

**Servings:** 16 slices

**Difficulty:** Intermediate

**Ingredients:**

- 5 1/3 cups wheat flour

- 1½ teaspoons salt

- 1½ tablespoons sugar

- 1 tablespoon dry yeast

- 1¾ cups water

- 2 tablespoons cumin

- 3 tablespoons sunflower oil

**Directions:**

1. Add warm water to the bread machine bucket.

2. Add salt, sugar, and sunflower oil.

3. Sift in wheat flour and add yeast.

4. Set the program of your bread machine to French bread and set crust type to Medium.

5. Once the maker beeps, add cumin.

6. Wait until the cycle completes.

7. Once the loaf is ready, take the bucket out and let the loaf cool for 5 minutes.

8. Gently shake the bucket to remove the loaf.

Nutrition:

Total Carbs: 67g

Fiber: 2g

Protein: 9.5g

Fat: 7g

Calories: 368

# 53. Potato Rosemary Loaf

**Preparation Time:** 5 minutes

**Cooking Time:** 3 hours and 25 minutes

**Servings:** 20 slices

**Difficulty:** Intermediate

**Ingredients:**

- 4 cups wheat flour

- 1 tablespoon sugar

- 1 tablespoon sunflower oil

- 1½ teaspoons salt

- 1½ cups water

- 1 teaspoon dry yeast

- 1 cup mashed potatoes, ground through a sieve

- crushed rosemary to taste

**Directions:**

1. Add flour, salt, and sugar to the bread maker bucket and attach mixing paddle.

2. Add sunflower oil and water.

3. Put in yeast as directed.

4. Set the program of your bread machine to Bread with Filling mode and set crust type to Medium.

5. Once the bread maker beeps and signals to add more ingredients, open lid, add mashed potatoes, and chopped rosemary.

6. Wait until the cycle completes.

7. Once the loaf is ready, take the bucket out and let the loaf cool for 5 minutes.

8. Gently shake the bucket to remove the loaf.

Nutrition:

Total Carbs: 54g

Fiber: 1g

Protein: 8g

Fat: 3g

Calories: 276

# 54. Delicious Honey Lavender Bread

**Preparation Time:** 10 minutes

**Cooking Time:** 3 hours and 25 minutes

**Servings:** 16 slices

**Difficulty:** Intermediate

**Ingredients:**

- 1½ cups wheat flour

- 2 1/3 cups whole meal flour

- 1 teaspoon fresh yeast

- 1½ cups water

- 1 teaspoon lavender

- 1½ tablespoons honey

- 1 teaspoon salt

**Directions:**

1. Sift both types of flour in a bowl and mix.

2. Add all of the ingredients to your bread machine, carefully following the instructions of the manufacturer.

3. Set the program of your bread machine to Basic/White Bread and set crust type to Medium.

4. Wait until the cycle completes.

5. Once the loaf is ready, take the bucket out and let the loaf cool for 5 minutes.

6. Gently shake the bucket to remove the loaf.

Nutrition:

Total Carbs: 46g

Fiber: 1g

Protein: 7.5g

Fat: 1.5g

Calories: 226

# 55. Inspiring Cinnamon Bread

**Preparation Time:** 15 minutes

**Cooking Time:** 2 hours and 15 minutes

**Servings:** 8 slices

**Difficulty:** Intermediate

**Ingredients:**

- 2/3 cup milk at 80 degrees F

- 1 whole egg, beaten

- 3 tablespoons melted butter, cooled

- 1/3 cup sugar

- 1/3 teaspoon salt

- 1 teaspoon ground cinnamon

- 2 cups white bread flour

- 1 1/3 teaspoons active dry yeast

**Directions:**

1. Add all of the ingredients to your bread machine, carefully following the instructions of the manufacturer.

2. Set the program of your bread machine to Basic/White Bread and set crust type to Medium.

3. Wait until the cycle completes.

4. Once the loaf is ready, take the bucket out and let the loaf cool for 5 minutes.

5. Remove the loaf

Nutrition:

Total Carbs: 34g

Fiber: 1g

Protein: 5g

Fat: 5g

Calories: 198

## 56. Lavender Buttermilk Bread

**Preparation time:** 10 minutes

**Cooking time:** 3 hours

**Servings:** 14

**Difficulty:** Expert

**Ingredients:**

- ½ cup water

- 7/8 cup buttermilk

- 1/4 cup olive oil

- 3 Tablespoon finely chopped fresh lavender leaves

- 1 ¼ teaspoon finely chopped fresh lavender flowers

- Grated zest of 1 lemon

- 4 cups bread flour

- 2 teaspoon salt

- 2 3/4 teaspoon bread machine yeast

**Directions:**

1. Add each ingredient to the bread machine in the order and at the temperature recommended by your bread machine manufacturer.

2. Close the lid, select the basic bread, medium crust setting on your bread machine and press start.

3. When the bread machine has finished baking, remove the bread and put it on a cooling rack.

Nutrition:

Carbs: 27 g

Fat: 5 g

Protein: 2 g

Calories: 170

# 57. Cajun Bread

**Preparation time:** 10 minutes

**Cooking time:** 2 hours 10 minutes

**Servings:** 14

**Difficulty:** Intermediate

**Ingredients:**

- ½ cup water

- ¼ cup chopped onion

- ¼ cup chopped green bell pepper

- 2 teaspoon finely chopped garlic

- 2 teaspoon soft butter

- 2 cups bread flour

- 1 Tablespoon sugar

- 1 teaspoon Cajun

- ½ teaspoon salt

- 1 teaspoon active dry yeast

Directions

1. Add each ingredient to the bread machine in the order and at the temperature recommended by your bread machine manufacturer.

2. Close the lid, select the basic bread, medium crust setting on your bread machine and press start.

3. When the bread machine has finished baking, remove the bread and put it on a cooling rack.

Nutrition:

Carbs: 23 g

Fat: 4 g

Protein: 5 g

Calories: 150

## 58. Turmeric Bread

**Preparation time:** 5 minutes

**Cooking time:** 3 hours

**Servings:** 14

**Difficulty:** Intermediate

**Ingredients:**

- 1 teaspoon dried yeast

- 4 cups strong white flour

- 1 teaspoon turmeric powder

- 2 teaspoon beetroot powder

- 2 Tablespoon olive oil

- 1.5 teaspoon salt

- 1 teaspoon chili flakes

- 1 3/8 water

**Directions:**

1. Add each ingredient to the bread machine in the order and at the temperature recommended by your bread machine manufacturer.

2. Close the lid, select the basic bread, medium crust setting on your bread machine and press start.

3. When the bread machine has finished baking, remove the bread and put it on a cooling rack.

Nutrition:

Carbs: 24 g

Fat: 3 g

Protein: 2 g

Calories: 129

# 59. Rosemary Cranberry Pecan Bread

**Preparation time:** 30 minutes

**Cooking time:** 3 hours

**Servings:** 14

**Difficulty:** Intermediate

**Ingredients:**

- 1 1/3 cups water, plus

- 2 Tablespoon water

- 2 Tablespoon butter

- 2 teaspoon salt

- 4 cups bread flour

- 3/4 cup dried sweetened cranberries

- 3/4 cup toasted chopped pecans

- 2 Tablespoon non-fat powdered milk

- ¼ cup sugar

- 2 teaspoon yeast

## Directions:

1. Add each ingredient to the bread machine in the order and at the temperature recommended by your bread machine manufacturer.

2. Close the lid, select the basic bread, medium crust setting on your bread machine and press start.

3. When the bread machine has finished baking, remove the bread and put it on a cooling rack.

Nutrition:

Carbs: 18 g

Fat: 5 g

Protein: 9 g

Calories: 120

# 60. Sesame French Bread

**Preparation time:** 20 minutes

**Cooking time:** 3 hours 15 minutes

**Servings:** 14

**Difficulty:** Intermediate

**Ingredients:**

- 7/8 cup water

- 1 Tablespoon butter, softened

- 3 cups bread flour

- 2 teaspoon sugar

- 1 teaspoon salt

- 2 teaspoon yeast

- 2 Tablespoon sesame seeds toasted

**Directions:**

1. Add each ingredient to the bread machine in the order and at the temperature recommended by your bread machine manufacturer.

2. Close the lid, select the French bread, medium crust setting on your bread machine and press start.

3. When the bread machine has finished baking, remove the bread and put it on a cooling rack.

Nutrition:

Carbs: 28 g

Fat: 3 g

Protein: 6 g

Calories: 180

## 61. Herb Bread

**Preparation Time:** 1 hour 20 minutes

**Cooking Time:** 50 minutes (20+30 minutes)

**Servings:** 1 loaf

**Difficulty:** Intermediate

**Ingredients:**

- 3/4 to 7/8 cup milk

- 1 tablespoon Sugar

- 1 teaspoon Salt

- tablespoon Butter or margarine

- 1/3 cup chopped onion

- cups bread flour

- 1/2 teaspoon Dried dill

- 1/2 teaspoon Dried basil

- 1/2 teaspoon Dried rosemary

- 11/2 teaspoon Active dry yeast

**Directions:**

1 Place all the Ingredients in the bread pan. Select medium crus then the rapid bake cycle. Press starts.

2 After 5-10 minutes, observe the dough as it kneads, if you hear straining sounds in your machine or if the dough appears stiff and dry, add 1 tablespoon Liquid at a time until the dough becomes smooth, pliable, soft, and slightly tacky to the touch.

3 Remove the bread from the pan after baking. Place on rack and allow to cool for 1 hour before slicing.

**Nutrition:**

Calories: 65 Cal

Fat     : 0 g

Carbohydrates: 13 g

Protein : 2 g

## 62. Rosemary Bread

**Preparation Time:** 2 hours 10 minutes

**Cooking Time:** 50 minutes

**Servings:** 1 loaf

**Difficulty:** Intermediate

**Ingredients:**

- ¾ cup + 1 tablespoon water at 80 degrees F
- 1⅔ tablespoons melted butter, cooled
- teaspoons sugar
- 1 teaspoon salt
- 1 tablespoon fresh rosemary, chopped
- cups white bread flour
- 1⅓ teaspoons instant yeast

**Directions:**

1. Add all of the ingredients to your bread machine, carefully following the instructions of the manufacturer.

2. Set the program of your bread machine to Basic/White Bread and set crust type to Medium.

3. Press START.

4. Wait until the cycle completes.

5. Once the loaf is ready, take the bucket out and let the loaf cool for 5 minutes.

6. Gently shake the bucket to remove the loaf.

7. Transfer to a cooling rack, slice, and serve.

**Nutrition:**

Calories: 142 Cal

Fat     : 3 g

Carbohydrates: 25 g

Protein : 4 g

Fiber: 1 g

### 63. Original Italian Herb Bread

**Preparation Time:** 2 hours 40 minutes

**Cooking Time:** 50 minutes

**Servings:** 2 loaves

**Difficulty:** Intermediate

**Ingredients:**

- 1 cup water at 80 degrees F

- ½ cup olive brine

- 1½ tablespoons butter

- tablespoons sugar

- teaspoons salt

- 5⅓ cups flour

- teaspoons bread machine yeast

- 20 olives, black/green

- 1½ teaspoons Italian herbs

**Directions:**

1    Cut olives into slices.

2    Add all of the ingredients to your bread machine (except olives), carefully following the instructions of the manufacturer.

3    Set the program of your bread machine to French bread and set crust type to Medium.

4    Press START.

5   Once the maker beeps, add olives.

6   Wait until the cycle completes.

7   Once the loaf is ready, take the bucket out and let the loaf cool for 5 minutes.

8   Gently shake the bucket to remove the loaf.

9   Transfer to a cooling rack, slice, and serve.

**Nutrition:**

Calories: 386 Cal

Fat     : 7 g

Carbohydrates: 71 g

Protein : 10 g

Fiber: 1 g

## 64. Lovely Aromatic Lavender Bread

**Preparation Time:** 2 hours 10 minutes

**Cooking Time:** 50 minutes

**Servings:** 1 loaf

**Difficulty:** Intermediate

**Ingredients:**

- ¾ cup milk at 80 degrees F

- 1 tablespoon melted butter, cooled

- 1 tablespoon sugar

- ¾ teaspoon salt

- 1 teaspoon fresh lavender flower, chopped

- ¼ teaspoon lemon zest

- ¼ teaspoon fresh thyme, chopped

- cups white bread flour

- ¾ teaspoon instant yeast

**Directions:**

1   Add all of the ingredients to your bread machine

2   Set the program of your bread machine to Basic/White Bread and set crust type to Medium.

3   Press START.

4   Wait until the cycle completes.

5   Once the loaf is ready, take the bucket out and let the loaf cool for 5 minutes.

6   Gently shake the bucket to remove the loaf.

7   Transfer to a cooling rack, slice, and serve.

**Nutrition:**

Calories: 144 Cal

Fat     : 2 g

Carbohydrates: 27 g

Protein : 4 g

Fiber: 1 g


## 65. Oregano Mozza-Cheese Bread

**Preparation Time:** 2 hours 50 minutes

**Cooking Time:** 50 minutes

**Servings:** 2 loaves

**Difficulty:** Intermediate

**Ingredients:**

- 1 cup (milk + egg) mixture
- ½ cup mozzarella cheese
- 2¼ cups flour
- ¾ cup whole grain flour
- tablespoons sugar
- 1 teaspoon salt
- teaspoons oregano
- 1½ teaspoons dry yeast

**Directions:**

1. Add all of the ingredients to your bread machine
2. Set the program of your bread machine to Basic/White Bread and set crust type to Dark.
3. Press START.
4. Wait until the cycle completes.
5. Once the loaf is ready, take the bucket out and let the loaf cool for 5 minutes.
6. Gently shake the bucket to remove the loaf.
7. Transfer to a cooling rack, slice, and serve.

**Nutrition:**

Calories: 209 Cal

Fat      : 2.1 g

Carbohydrates: 40 g

Protein: 7.7 g

Fiber: 1 g

## 66. Garlic Bread

**Preparation Time:** 2 hours 30 minutes

**Cooking Time:** 40 minutes

**Servings:** 1 loaf

**Difficulty:** Intermediate

**Ingredients:**

- 1 3/8 cups water

- tablespoons olive oil

- 1 teaspoon minced garlic

- cups bread flour

- tablespoons white sugar

- teaspoons salt

- 1/4 cup grated Parmesan cheese

- 1 teaspoon dried basil

- 1 teaspoon garlic powder

- tablespoons chopped fresh chives

- 1 teaspoon coarsely ground black pepper

- 1/2 teaspoons bread machine yeast

## Directions:

1   Follow the order of putting the ingredients into the pan of the bread machine recommended by the manufacturer.

2   Choose the Basic or the White Bread cycle on the machine and press the Start button.

## Nutrition:

Calories: 175 calories;

Total Carbohydrate: 29.7 g

Cholesterol: 1 mg

Total Fat: 3.7 g

Protein: 5.2 g

Sodium: 332 mg

## 67. Rosemary Bread

**Preparation Time:** 2 hours 40 minutes

**Cooking Time:** 25- 30 minutes

**Servings:** 1 loaf

**Difficulty:** Intermediate

**Ingredients:**

- 1 cup water

- tablespoons olive oil

- 1 1/2 teaspoons white sugar

- 1 1/2 teaspoons salt

- 1/4 teaspoon Italian seasoning

- 1/4 teaspoon ground black pepper

- 1 tablespoon dried rosemary

- 1/2 cups bread flour

- 1 1/2 teaspoons active dry yeast

## Directions:

1   Into the bread machine pan, put the ingredients following the order recommended by manufacturer.

2   Use the white bread cycle and then push the Start button.

## Nutrition:

Calories: 137 calories;

Total Carbohydrate: 21.6 g

Cholesterol: 0 mg

Total Fat: 3.9 g

Protein: 3.6 g

Sodium: 292 mg

## 68. Cumin Bread

**Preparation Time:** 3 hours 30 minutes

**Cooking Time:** 15 minutes

**Servings:** 8

**Difficulty:** Intermediate

**Ingredients:**

- 1/3 cups bread machine flour, sifted

- 1½ teaspoon kosher salt

- 1½ Tablespoon sugar

- 1 Tablespoon bread machine yeast

- 1¾ cups lukewarm water

- Tablespoon black cumin

- Tablespoon sunflower oil

**Directions:**

1   Place all the dry and liquid ingredients in the pan and follow the instructions for your bread machine.

2   Set the baking program to BASIC and the crust type to MEDIUM.

3   If the dough is too dense or too wet, adjust the amount of flour and liquid in the recipe.

4   When the program has ended, take the pan out of the bread machine and let cool for 5 minutes.

5   Shake the loaf out of the pan. If necessary, use a spatula.

6   Wrap the bread with a kitchen towel and set it aside for an hour. Otherwise, you can cool it on a wire rack.

**Nutrition:**

Calories: 368 calories;

Total Carbohydrate: 67.1 g

Cholesterol: 0 mg

Total Fat: 6.5 g

Protein: 9.5 g

Sodium: 444 mg

Sugar: 2.5 g

## 69. Saffron Tomato Bread

**Preparation Time:** 3 hours 30 minutes

**Cooking Time:** 15 minutes

**Servings:** 10

**Difficulty:** Intermediate

**Ingredients:**

- 1 teaspoon bread machine yeast
- 2½ cups wheat bread machine flour
- 1 Tablespoon panifarin
- 1½ teaspoon kosher salt
- 1½ Tablespoon white sugar
- Tablespoon extra-virgin olive oil
- Tablespoon tomatoes, dried and chopped
- 1 Tablespoon tomato paste
- ½ cup firm cheese (cubes)
- ½ cup feta cheese
- 1 pinch saffron
- 1½ cups serum

**Directions:**

1    Five minutes before cooking, pour in dried tomatoes and 1 tablespoon of olive oil. Add the tomato paste and mix.

2    Place all the dry and liquid ingredients, except additives, in the pan and follow the instructions for your bread machine.

3    Pay particular attention to measuring the ingredients. Use a measuring cup, measuring spoon, and kitchen scales to do so.

4    Set the baking program to BASIC and the crust type to MEDIUM.

5    Add the additives after the beep or place them in the dispenser of the bread machine.

6    Shake the loaf out of the pan. If necessary, use a spatula.

7    Wrap the bread with a kitchen towel and set it aside for an hour. Otherwise, you can cool it on a wire rack.

**Nutrition:**

Calories: 260 calories;

Total Carbohydrate: 35.5 g

Cholesterol: 20 g

Total Fat: 9.2g

Protein: 8.9 g

Sodium: 611 mg

Sugar: 5.2 g

## 70. Cracked Black Pepper Bread

**Preparation Time:** 3 hours 30 minutes

**Cooking Time:** 15 minutes

**Servings:** 8

**Difficulty:** Intermediate

**Ingredients:**

- ¾ cup water, at 80°F to 90°F

- 1 tablespoon melted butter, cooled

- 1 tablespoon sugar

- ¾ teaspoon salt

- tablespoons skim milk powder

- 1 tablespoon minced chives

- ½ teaspoon garlic powder

- ½ teaspoon cracked black pepper

- cups white bread flour

- ¾ teaspoon bread machine or instant yeast

**Directions:**

1  Place the ingredients in your bread machine as recommended by the manufacturer.

2  Program the machine for Basic/White bread, select light or medium crust, and press Start.

3  When the loaf is done, remove the bucket from the machine.

4  Let the loaf cool for 5 minutes.

5  Gently shake the bucket to remove the loaf, and turn it out onto a rack to cool.

**Nutrition:**

Calories: 141 calories;

Total Carbohydrate: 27 g

Total Fat: 2g

Protein: 4 g

Sodium: 215 mg

Fiber: 1 g

## 71. Spicy Cajun Bread

**Preparation Time:** 2 hours

**Cooking Time:** 15 minutes

**Servings:** 8

**Difficulty:** Intermediate

**Ingredients:**

- ¾ cup water, at 80°F to 90°F

- 1 tablespoon melted butter, cooled

- teaspoons tomato paste

- 1 tablespoon sugar

- 1 teaspoon salt

- tablespoons skim milk powder

- ½ tablespoon Cajun seasoning

- ⅛ teaspoon onion powder

- cups white bread flour

- 1 teaspoon bread machine or instant yeast

**Directions:**

1  Place the ingredients in your bread machine as recommended by the manufacturer.

2  Program the machine for Basic/White bread, select light or medium crust, and press Start.

3    When the loaf is done, remove the bucket from the machine.

4    Let the loaf cool for 5 minutes.

5    Gently shake the bucket to remove the loaf, and turn it out onto a rack to cool.

**Nutrition:**

Calories: 141 calories;

Total Carbohydrate: 27 g

Total Fat: 2g

Protein: 4 g

Sodium: 215 mg

Fiber: 1 g

## 72. Anise Lemon Bread

**Preparation Time:** 2 hours

**Cooking Time:** 15 minutes

**Servings:** 8

**Difficulty:** Intermediate

**Ingredients:**

- ⅔ Cup water, at 80°F to 90°F

- 1 egg, at room temperature

- 2⅔ tablespoons butter, melted and cooled

- 2⅔ tablespoons honey

- ⅓ Teaspoon salt

- ⅔ Teaspoon anise seed

- ⅔ Teaspoon lemon zest

- cups white bread flour

- 1⅓ teaspoons bread machine or instant yeast

**Directions:**

1. Place the ingredients in your bread machine as recommended by the manufacturer.

2. Program the machine for Basic/White bread, select light or medium crust, and press Start.

3. When the loaf is done, remove the bucket from the machine.

4. Let the loaf cool for 5 minutes.

5. Gently shake the bucket to remove the loaf, and turn it out onto a rack to cool.

**Nutrition:**

Calories: 158 calories;

Total Carbohydrate: 27 g

Total Fat: 5g

Protein: 4 g

Sodium: 131 mg

Fiber: 1 g

## 73. Cardamon Bread

**Preparation Time:** 2 hours

**Cooking Time:** 15 minutes

**Servings:** 8

**Difficulty:** Intermediate

**Ingredients:**

- ½ cup milk, at 80°F to 90°F

- 1 egg, at room temperature

- 1 teaspoon melted butter, cooled

- teaspoons honey

- ⅔ Teaspoon salt

- ⅔ Teaspoon ground cardamom

- cups white bread flour

- ¾ teaspoon bread machine or instant yeast

**Directions:**

1. Place the ingredients in your bread machine as recommended by the manufacturer.

2. Program the machine for Basic/White bread, select light or medium crust, and press Start.

3. When the loaf is done, remove the bucket from the machine.

4. Let the loaf cool for 5 minutes.

5. Gently shake the bucket to remove the loaf, and turn it out onto a rack to cool.

**Nutrition:**

Calories: 149 calories;

Total Carbohydrate: 29 g

Total Fat: 2g

Protein: 5 g

Sodium: 211 mg

Fiber: 1 g

# Chapter 9.   Fruit Breads

### 74. Banana Bread

**Preparation Time:** 1 hour 40 minutes

**Cooking Time:** 40- 45 minutes

**Servings:** 1 loaf

**Difficulty:** Beginners

**Ingredients:**

- 1 teaspoon Baking powder

- 1/2 teaspoon Baking soda

- bananas, peeled and halved lengthwise

- cups all-purpose flour

- eggs

- tablespoon Vegetable oil

- 3/4 cup white sugar

**Directions:**

1   Put all the Ingredients in the bread pan. Select dough setting. Start and mix for about 3-5 minutes.

2   After 3-5 minutes, press stop. Do not continue to mix. Smooth out the top of the dough

3   Using the spatula and then select bake, start and bake for about 50 minutes. After 50 minutes, insert a toothpick into the top center to test doneness.

4   Remove bread and cool in wire rack.

**Nutrition:**

Calories: 310 calories

Total Carbohydrate: 40 g

Fat: 13 g

Protein: 3 g

## 75. Blueberry Bread

**Preparation Time:** 3 hours 15 minutes

**Cooking Time:** 40- 45 minutes

**Servings:** 1 loaf

**Difficulty:** Beginners

**Ingredients:**

- 1⅛ to 1¼ cups Water
- ounces Cream cheese, softened
- tablespoons Butter or margarine
- ¼ cup Sugar
- teaspoons Salt
- 4½ cups Bread flour
- 1½ teaspoons Grated lemon peel
- teaspoons Cardamom
- tablespoons Nonfat dry milk
- 2½ teaspoons Red star brand active dry yeast
- ⅔ cup dried blueberries

**Directions:**

1   Place all Ingredients except dried blueberries in bread pan, using the least amount of liquid listed in the recipe. Select light crust setting and raisin/nut cycle. Press starts.

2   Observe the dough as it kneads. After 5 to 10 minutes, if it appears dry and stiff or if your ma- chine sounds as if it's straining to knead it, add more liquid 1 tablespoon at a time until dough forms a smooth, soft, pliable ball that is slightly tacky to the touch.

3   At the beep, add the dried blueberries.

4   After the baking cycle ends, remove bread from pan, place on cake rack, and allow to cool 1 hour before slicing.

**Nutrition:**

Calories: 180 calories

Total Carbohydrate: 250 g

Fat: 3 g

Protein: 9 g

## 76. Orange and Walnut Bread

**Preparation Time:** 2 hours 50 minutes

**Cooking Time:** 45 minutes

**Servings:** 10- 15

**Difficulty:** Beginners

**Ingredients:**

1 egg white

- 1 tablespoon water

- ½ cup warm whey

- 1 tablespoons yeast

- tablespoons sugar

- oranges, crushed

- cups flour

- 1 teaspoon salt

- 1 and ½ tablespoon salt

- teaspoons orange peel

- 1/3 teaspoon vanilla

- tablespoons walnut and almonds, crushed

- Crushed pepper, salt, cheese for garnish

## Directions:

1  Add all of the ingredients to your Bread Machine (except egg white, 1 tablespoon water and crushed pepper/ cheese).

2  Set the program to "Dough" cycle and let the cycle run.

3  Remove the dough (using lightly floured hands) and carefully place it on a floured surface.

4  Cover with a light film/cling paper and let the dough rise for 10 minutes.

5  Divide the dough into thirds after it has risen

6  Place on a lightly flour surface, roll each portion into 14x10 inch sized rectangles

7  Use a sharp knife to cut carefully cut the dough into strips of ½ inch width

8  Pick 2-3 strips and twist them multiple times, making sure to press the ends together

9  Preheat your oven to 400 degrees F

10  Take a bowl and stir egg white, water and brush onto the breadsticks

11  Sprinkle salt, pepper/ cheese

12  Bake for 10-12 minutes until golden brown

13  Remove from baking sheet and transfer to cooling rack Serve and enjoy!

## Nutrition:

Calories: 437 calories;

Total Carbohydrate: 82 g

Total Fat: 7 g

Protein: 12 g

Sugar: 34 g

Fiber: 1 g

## 77. Lemon and Poppy Buns

**Preparation Time:** 2 hours 50 minutes

**Cooking Time:** 45 minutes

**Servings:** 10- 20 buns

**Difficulty:** Beginners

**Ingredients:**

- Melted Butter for grease

- 1 and 1/3 cups hot water

- tablespoons powdered milk

- tablespoons Crisco shortening

- 1 and ½ teaspoon salt

- 1 tablespoon lemon juice

- and ¼ cups bread flour

- ½ teaspoon nutmeg

- teaspoons grated lemon rind

- tablespoons poppy seeds

- 1 and ¼ teaspoons yeast

- teaspoons wheat gluten

**Directions:**

1   Add all of the ingredients to your Bread Machine (except melted butter).

2   Set the program to "Dough" cycle and let the cycle run.

3   Remove the dough (using lightly floured hands) and carefully place it on a floured surface.

4   Cover with a light film/cling paper and let the dough rise for 10 minutes.

5   Take a large cookie sheet and grease with butter.

6   Cut the risen dough into 15-20 pieces and shape them into balls.

7   Place the balls onto the sheet (2 inches apart) and cover.

8   Place in a warm place and let them rise for 30-40 minutes until the dough doubles.

9   Preheat your oven to 375 degrees F, transfer the cookie sheet to your oven and bake for 12-15 minutes. Brush the top with a bit of butter, enjoy!

**Nutrition:**

Calories: 231 calories;

Total Carbohydrate: 31 g

Total Fat: 11 g

Protein: 4 g

Sugar: 12 g

Fiber: 1 g

## 78. Apple with Pumpkin Bread

**Preparation Time:** 2 hours 50 minutes

**Cooking Time:** 45 minutes

**Servings:** 2 loaves

**Difficulty:** Beginners

**Ingredients:**

- 1/3 cup dried apples, chopped
- 1 1/2 teaspoon bread machine yeast
- cups bread flour
- 1/3 cup ground pecans
- 1/4 teaspoon ground nutmeg
- 1/4 teaspoon ground ginger
- 1/4 teaspoon allspice
- 1/2 teaspoon ground cinnamon
- 1 1/4 teaspoon salt
- tablespoon unsalted butter, cubed
- 1/3 cup dry skim milk powder
- 1/4 cup honey
- large eggs, at room temperature
- 2/3 cup pumpkin puree
- 2/3 cup water, with a temperature of 80 to 90 degrees F (26 to 32 degrees C)

**Directions:**

1   Put all ingredients, except the dried apples, in the bread pan in this order: water, pumpkin puree, eggs, honey, skim milk, butter, salt, allspice, cinnamon, pecans, nutmeg, ginger, flour, and yeast.

2   Secure the pan in the machine and lock the lid.

3   Place the dried apples in the fruit and nut dispenser.

4    Turn on the machine. Choose the sweet setting and your desired color of the crust.

5    Carefully unmold the baked bread once done and allow to cool for 20 minutes before slicing.

**Nutrition:**

Calories: 228 calories;

Total Carbohydrate: 30 g

Total Fat: 4 g

Protein: 18 g

## 79. Peaches and Cream Bread

**Preparation Time:** 2 hours

**Cooking Time:** 15 minutes

**Servings:** 8

**Difficulty:** Beginners

**Ingredients:**

- ½ cup canned peaches, drained and chopped
- ¼ cup heavy whipping cream, at 80°F to 90°F
- 1 egg, at room temperature
- ¾ tablespoon melted butter, cooled
- 1½ tablespoons sugar
- ¾ teaspoon salt
- ¼ teaspoon ground cinnamon
- ⅛ teaspoon ground nutmeg

- ¼ cup whole-wheat flour

- 1¾ cups white bread flour

- ¾ teaspoons bread machine or instant yeast

## Directions:

1   Place the ingredients in your bread machine as recommended by the manufacturer.

2   Program the machine for Basic/White bread, select light or medium crust, and press Start.

3   When the loaf is done, remove the bucket from the machine.

4   Let the loaf cool for 5 minutes.

5   Gently shake the bucket to remove the loaf, and turn it out onto a rack to cool.

## Nutrition:

Calories: 153 calories;

Total Carbohydrate: 27 g

Total Fat: 4 g

Protein: 5 g

Sodium: 208 mg

Fiber: 1 g

## 80. Warm Spiced Pumpkin Bread

**Preparation Time:** 2 hours

**Cooking Time:** 15 minutes

**Servings:** 12- 16

**Difficulty:** Beginners

**Ingredients:**

- Butter for greasing the bucket

- 1½ cups pumpkin purée

- eggs, at room temperature

- ⅓ cup melted butter, cooled

- 1 cup sugar

- cups all-purpose flour

- 1½ teaspoons baking powder

- ¾ teaspoon ground cinnamon

- ½ teaspoon baking soda

- ¼ teaspoon ground nutmeg

- ¼ teaspoon ground ginger

- ¼ teaspoon salt

- Pinch ground cloves

**Directions:**

1  Lightly grease the bread bucket with butter.

2  Add the pumpkin, eggs, butter, and sugar.

3  Program the machine for Quick/Rapid bread and press Start.

4  Let the wet ingredients be mixed by the paddles until the first fast mixing cycle is finished, about 10 minutes into the cycle.

5  When the loaf is done, remove the bucket from the machine.

6  Let the loaf cool for 5 minutes.

7  Gently shake the bucket to remove the loaf, and turn it out onto a rack to cool.

**Nutrition:**

Calories: 251 calories;

Total Carbohydrate: 43 g

Total Fat: 7 g

Protein: 5 g

Sodium: 159 mg

Fiber: 2 g

## 81. Pure Peach Bread

**Preparation Time:** 2 hours

**Cooking Time:** 15 minutes

**Servings:** 12

**Difficulty:** Beginners

**Ingredients:**

- ¾ cup peaches, chopped

- ⅓ cup heavy whipping cream

- 1 egg

- 1 tablespoon butter, melted at room temperature

- ⅓ teaspoon ground cinnamon

- ⅛ teaspoon ground nutmeg

- ¼ tablespoons sugar

- 1 ⅛ teaspoons salt

- ⅓ cup whole-wheat flour

- ⅔ cups white bread flour

- 1 ⅛ teaspoons instant or bread machine yeast

**Directions:**

1 Take 1 ½ pound size loaf pan and first add the liquid ingredients and then add the dry ingredients.

2 Place the loaf pan in the machine and close its top lid.

3 For selecting a bread cycle, press "Basic Bread/White Bread/Regular Bread" and for selecting a crust type, press "Light" or "Medium".

4 Start the machine and it will start preparing the bread.

5 After the bread loaf is completed, open the lid and take out the loaf pan.

6 Allow the pan to cool down for 10-15 minutes on a wire rack. Gently shake the pan and remove the bread loaf.

7 Make slices and serve.

**Nutrition:**

Calories: 51 calories;

Total Carbohydrate: 12 g

Cholesterol: 0 g

Total Fat: 0.3 g

Protein: 1.20 g

Fiber: 2 g

## 82. Date Delight Bread

**Preparation Time:** 2 hours

**Cooking Time:** 15 minutes

**Servings:** 12

**Difficulty:** Beginners

**Ingredients:**

- ¾ cup water, lukewarm
- ½ cup milk, lukewarm
- tablespoons butter, melted at room temperature
- ¼ cup honey
- tablespoons molasses
- 1 tablespoon sugar
- ¼ cups whole-wheat flour
- 1 ¼ cups white bread flour
- tablespoons skim milk powder
- 1 teaspoon salt
- 1 tablespoon unsweetened cocoa powder
- 1 ½ teaspoons instant or bread machine yeast
- ¾ cup chopped dates

**Directions:**

1 Take 1 ½ pound size loaf pan and first add the liquid ingredients and then add the dry ingredients. (Do not add the dates as of now.)

2 Place the loaf pan in the machine and close its top lid.

3 Plug the bread machine into power socket. For selecting a bread cycle, press "Basic Bread/White Bread/Regular Bread" or "Fruit/Nut Bread" and for selecting a crust type, press "Light" or "Medium".

4   Start the machine and it will start preparing the bread. When machine beeps or signals, add the dates.

5   After the bread loaf is completed, open the lid and take out the loaf pan.

6   Allow the pan to cool down for 10-15 minutes on a wire rack. Gently shake the pan and remove the bread loaf.

7   Make slices and serve.

**Nutrition:**

Calories: 220 calories;

Total Carbohydrate: 52 g

Cholesterol: 0 g

Total Fat: 5 g

Protein: 4 g

## 83. Blueberry Honey Bread

**Preparation Time:** 2 hours

**Cooking Time:** 15 minutes

**Servings:** 12

**Difficulty:** Beginners

**Ingredients:**

- ¾ cup milk, lukewarm
- 1 egg, at room temperature
- ¼ tablespoons butter, melted at room temperature
- 1 ½ tablespoons honey

- ½ cup rolled oats

- ⅓ cups white bread flour

- 1 ⅛ teaspoons salt

- 1 ½ teaspoons instant or bread machine yeast

- ½ cup dried blueberries

**Directions:**

1  Take 1 ½ pound size loaf pan and first add the liquid ingredients and then add the dry ingredients. (Do not add the blueberries as of now.)

2  Place the loaf pan in the machine and close its top lid.

3  Plug the bread machine into power socket. For selecting a bread cycle, press "Basic Bread/White Bread/Regular Bread" or "Fruit/Nut Bread" and for selecting a crust type, press "Light" or "Medium".

4  Start the machine and it will start preparing the bread. When machine beeps or signals, add the blueberries.

5  After the bread loaf is completed, open the lid and take out the loaf pan.

6  Allow the pan to cool down for 10-15 minutes on a wire rack. Gently shake the pan and remove the bread loaf.

Make slices and serve.

**Nutrition:**

Calories: 180 calories;

Total Carbohydrate: 250 g

Total Fat: 3 g

Protein: 9 g

# Chapter 10.   Grain, Seed And Nut Bread

## 84. Oat Bread

**Preparation Time**: 1 hour 30 minutes

**Cooking Time:** 40 minutes

**Servings:** 2-3 loaves

**Difficulty:** Beginners

**Ingredients:**

- 1 cup Oats
- 1⅜ to 1½ cups Water
- tablespoons Butter or margarine
- ¼ cup Honey
- teaspoons Salt
- cups Bread flour red star brand
- 2½ teaspoons Active dry yeast

**Directions:**

1   Place all Ingredients in bread pan, using the least amount of liquid listed in the recipe. Select medium crust setting and press start.

2   Observe the dough as it kneads. After 5 to 10 minutes, if it appears dry and stiff or if your machine sounds as if it's straining to knead it, add more liquid 1 tablespoon at a time until dough forms a smooth, soft, pliable ball that is slightly tacky to the touch.

3   After the baking cycle ends, remove bread from pan, place on cake rack, and allow to cool 1 hour before slicing.

**Nutrition**:

Calories: 110 Cal

Carbohydrate: 19 g

Fat: 2 g

Protein: 4 g

## 85. Whole-Wheat Bread

**Preparation Time**: 1 hour 10 minutes

**Cooking Time:** 40 minutes

**Servings:** 1 loaf

**Difficulty:** Beginners

**Ingredients:**

- 3/4 to 7/8 cup water
- 1 teaspoon Salt
- tablespoon Butter or margarine
- 1 tablespoon Sugar
- 11/3 cups whole wheat flour
- 2/3 cups bread flour
- tablespoon Instant potato flakes
- 11/2 teaspoon Active dry yeast optional:
- tablespoon vital wheat gluten

**Directions:**

1   Using the least amount of the liquid indicated in the recipe, place all the Ingredients in the bread pan. Select medium crust then the whole wheat cycle. Press starts.

2   After 5-10 minutes, observe the dough as it kneads, if you hear straining sounds in your machine or if the dough appears stiff and dry, add 1 tablespoon Liquid at a time until the dough becomes smooth, pliable, soft, and slightly tacky to the touch.

3   Remove the bread from the pan after baking. Place on rack and allow to cool for 1 hour before slicing.

**Nutrition:**

Calories: 60 Cal

Carbohydrate: 11 g

Fat: 1 g

Protein: 3 g

## 86. Awesome Golden Corn Bread

**Preparation Time:** 1 hour 10 minutes

**Cooking Time:** 50 minutes

**Servings:** 2 loaves

**Difficulty:** Beginners

**Ingredients:**

- 1 cup buttermilk at 80 degrees F
- whole eggs, at room temperature
- ¼ cup melted butter, cooled
- 1⅓ cups all-purpose flour
- 1 cup cornmeal

- ¼ cup sugar

- 1 tablespoon baking powder

- 1 teaspoon salt

**Directions:**

1  Add buttermilk, butter, and eggs to your bread machine, carefully following the manufacturer instructions.

2  Program the machine for Quick/Rapid Bread mode and press START.

3  While the wet ingredients are being mixed in the machine, take a small bowl and combine it in flour, cornmeal, sugar, baking powder, and salt.

4  After the first fast mix is done and the machine gives the signal, add dry ingredients.

5  Wait until the whole cycle completes.

6  Once the loaf is done, take the bucket out and let it cool for 5 minutes.

7  Gently shake the basket to remove the loaf and transfer to a cooling rack.

8  Slice and serve!

**Nutrition:**

Calories: 158 Cal

Fat      : 5 g

Carbohydrates: 24 g

Protein : 4 g

Fiber: 2 g

## 87. Hearty Oatmeal Bread

**Preparation Time:** 2 hours 10 minutes

**Cooking Time:** 50 minutes

**Servings:** 1 loaf

**Difficulty:** Beginners

**Ingredients:**

- ¾ cup water at 80 degrees F
- tablespoons melted butter, cooled
- tablespoons sugar
- 1 teaspoon salt
- ¾ cup quick oats
- 1½ cups white bread flour
- 1 teaspoon instant yeast

**Directions:**

1   Add all of the ingredients to your bread machine, carefully following the instructions of the manufacturer.

2   Set the program of your bread machine to Basic/White Bread and set crust type to Medium.

3   Press START.

4   Wait until the cycle completes.

5   Once the loaf is ready, take the bucket out and let the loaf cool for 5 minutes.

6   Gently shake the bucket to remove the loaf.

7   Transfer to a cooling rack, slice, and serve.

**Nutrition:**

Calories: 149 Cal

Fat     : 4 g

Carbohydrates: 26 g

Protein : 4 g

Fiber: 1 g

## 88. Corn, Poppy Seeds and Sour Cream Bread

**Preparation Time:** 2 hours 40 minutes

**Cooking Time:** 50 minutes

**Servings:** 2 loaves

**Difficulty:** Beginners

**Ingredients:**

- 3½ cups wheat flour

- 1¾ cups corn flour

- ounces sour cream

- tablespoons corn oil

- teaspoons active dried yeast

- teaspoons salt

- 16 ¼ ounces water

- Poppy seeds for sprinkling

**Directions:**

1. Add 16¼ ounces of water and corn oil to the bread maker bucket.

2. Add flour, sour cream, sugar, and salt from different angles.

3. Make a groove in the flour and add yeast.

4.      Set the program of your bread machine to Basic/White Bread and set crust type to Medium.

5.      Press START.

6.      Wait until the cycle completes.

7.      Once the loaf is ready, take the bucket out and let the loaf cool for 5 minutes.

8.      Gently shake the bucket to remove the loaf.

9.      Moisten the surface with water and sprinkle with poppy seeds.

10.     Transfer to a cooling rack, slice, and serve.

**Nutrition:**

Calories: 374 Cal

Fat      : 10 g

Carbohydrates: 64 g

Protein : 9 g

Fiber: 1 g

## 89. Grampy's Special Bread

**Preparation Time:** 2 hours 30 minutes

**Cooking Time:** 40 minutes

**Servings:** 1 loaf

**Difficulty:** Beginners

**Ingredients:**

- 1 1/4 cups skim milk

- 1 cup crispy rice cereal

- cups bread flour

- tablespoons honey

- 1 1/4 teaspoons salt

- 1 1/2 (.25 oz.) packages active dry yeast

- tablespoons margarine

## Directions:

1   Into the bread machine pan, add the ingredients according to the order given by manufacturer. Use Basic/White Bread setting and then press the Start button.

## Nutrition:

Calories: 46 calories;

Total Carbohydrate: 6.5 g

Cholesterol: < 1 mg

Total Fat: 1.9 g

Protein: 1.4 g

Sodium: 292 mg

## 90. Butter Honey Wheat Bread

**Preparation Time:** 3 hours 5 minutes

**Cooking Time:** 15 minutes

**Servings:** 12

**Difficulty:** Beginners

**Ingredients:**

1 cup water

- tablespoons margarine

- tablespoons honey

- cups bread flour

- 1/2 cup whole wheat flour

- 1/3 cup dry milk powder

- 1 teaspoon salt

- 1 (.25 oz.) package active dry yeast

## Directions:

2   Follow the order of putting the ingredients into the bread machine recommended by the manufacturer. Run the bread machine for large loaf (1-1/2 lb.) on Wheat setting.

## Nutrition:

Calories: 57 calories;

Total Carbohydrate: 8.5 g

Cholesterol: < 1 mg

Total Fat: 1.9 g

Protein: 2.1 g

Sodium: 234 mg

## 91. Buttermilk Wheat Bread

**Preparation Time:** 6 hours 8 minutes

**Cooking Time:** 15 minutes

**Servings:** 12

**Difficulty:** Beginners

## Ingredients:

- 1 1/2 cups buttermilk
- 1 1/2 tablespoons butter, melted
- tablespoons white sugar
- 3/4 teaspoon salt
- cups all-purpose flour
- 1/3 cup whole wheat flour
- 1 1/2 teaspoons active dry yeast

## Directions:

1  In the bread machine pan, measure all ingredients in the order the manufacturer recommended. Set the machine to the Basic White Bread setting.

2  Start the machine. After a few minutes, add more buttermilk if the ingredients do not form a ball, or if it is too loose, put a handful of flour.

## Nutrition:

Calories: 160 calories;

Total Carbohydrate: 30 g

Cholesterol: 5 mg

Total Fat: 2.1 g

Protein: 4.9 g

Sodium: 189 mg

## 92. Cracked Wheat Bread

**Preparation Time:** 3 hours 5 minutes

**Cooking Time:** 15 minutes

**Servings:** 12

**Difficulty:** Beginners

**Ingredients:**

- 1 1/4 cups water
- tablespoons margarine, softened
- tablespoons dry milk powder
- tablespoons brown sugar
- 1 1/4 teaspoons salt
- cups bread flour
- 1/3 cup whole wheat flour
- 1/4 cup cracked wheat
- 1 1/4 teaspoons active dry yeast

**Directions:**

1  In bread machine pan, measure all of the ingredients in the order the manufacturer suggested. Choose regular/light cycle; then start.

**Nutrition:**

Calories: 50 calories;

Total Carbohydrate: 7.3 g

Cholesterol: < 1 mg

Total Fat: 1.9 g

Protein: 1.4 g

Sodium: 271 mg

Sodium: 189 mg

## 93. Flax and Sunflower Seed Bread

**Preparation Time:** 3 hours

**Cooking Time:** 15 minutes

**Servings:** 15

**Difficulty:** Beginners

**Ingredients:**

- 1 1/3 cups water
- tablespoons butter, softened
- tablespoons honey
- 1 1/2 cups bread flour
- 1 1/3 cups whole wheat bread flour
- 1 teaspoon salt
- 1 teaspoon active dry yeast
- 1/2 cup flax seeds
- 1/2 cup sunflower seeds

**Directions:**

1  With suggested order by manufacturer, add the all ingredients, (apart from sunflower seeds) in pan of bread machine.

2  Select basic white cycle; press start. Just in the knead cycle that your machine signals alert sounds, add the sunflower seeds.

**Nutrition:**

Calories: 140 calories;

Total Carbohydrate: 22.7 g

Cholesterol: 4 mg

Total Fat: 4.2 g

Protein: 4.2 g

Sodium: 169 mg

## 94. High Flavor Bran Bread

**Preparation Time:** 3 hours

**Cooking Time:** 15 minutes

**Servings:** 15

**Difficulty:** Beginners

**Ingredients:**

- 1 1/2 cups warm water (110 degrees F/45 degrees C)
- tablespoons dry milk powder
- tablespoons vegetable oil
- tablespoons molasses
- tablespoons honey
- 1 1/2 teaspoons salt
- 1/4 cups whole wheat flour
- 1 1/4 cups bread flour
- 1 cup whole bran cereal
- teaspoons active dry yeast

**Directions:**

1   In the pan of your bread machine, add the ingredients in the directed by the machine's maker.

2   Set the machine to either the whole grain or whole wheat setting.

**Nutrition:**

Calories: 146 calories;

Total Carbohydrate: 27.9 g

Cholesterol: < 1 mg

Total Fat: 2.4 g

Protein: 4.6 g

Sodium: 254 mg

## 95. Honey and Flaxseed Bread

**Preparation Time:** 3 hours

**Cooking Time:** 15 minutes

**Servings:** 12

**Difficulty:** Expert

**Ingredients:**

- 1 1/8 cups water

- 1 1/2 tablespoons flaxseed oil

- tablespoons honey

- 1/2 tablespoon liquid lecithin

- cups whole wheat flour

- 1/2 cup flax seed

- tablespoons bread flour

- tablespoons whey powder

- 1 1/2 teaspoons sea salt

- teaspoons active dry yeast

**Directions:**

1  In the bread machine pan, put in all of the ingredients following the order recommended by the manufacturer.

2  Choose the Wheat cycle on the machine and press the Start button to run the machine.

**Nutrition:**

Calories: 174 calories;

Total Carbohydrate: 30.8 g

Cholesterol: < 1 mg

Total Fat: 4.9 g

Protein: 7.1 g

Sodium: 242 mg

## 96. Honey Whole Wheat Bread

**Preparation Time:** 3 hours 5 minutes

**Cooking Time:** 15 minutes

**Servings:** 10

**Difficulty:** Beginners

**Ingredients:**

- 1 1/8 cups warm water (110 degrees F/45 degrees C)

- tablespoons honey

- 1/3 teaspoon salt

- 1 1/2 cups whole wheat flour

- 1 1/2 cups bread flour

- tablespoons vegetable oil

- 1 1/2 teaspoons active dry yeast

**Directions:**

1　Put the ingredients into the bread machine following the order recommended by the manufacturer.

2　Choose the Wheat Bread cycle and the setting for Light Color on the machine.

**Nutrition:**

Calories: 180 calories;

Total Carbohydrate: 33.4 g

Cholesterol: 0 mg

Total Fat: 3.5 g

Protein: 5.2 g

Sodium: 79 mg

## 97. Maple Whole Wheat Bread

**Preparation Time:** 3 hours 5 minutes

**Cooking Time:** 15 minutes

**Servings:** 10

**Difficulty:** Beginners

**Ingredients:**

- 1/2 cups whole wheat flour
- 1/2 cup bread flour
- 1/3 teaspoon salt
- 1 1/4 cups water
- tablespoons maple syrup
- tablespoons olive oil
- 1 1/2 teaspoons active dry yeast

**Directions:**

1   Put the ingredients into the bread machine pan following the order suggested by the manufacturer.

2   Choose the Wheat Bread cycle on the machine and press the Start button.

**Nutrition:**

Calories: 144 calories;

Total Carbohydrate: 26.9 g

Cholesterol: 0 mg

Total Fat: 2.8 g

Protein: 4.3 g

Sodium: 67 mg

## 98. Oat and Honey Bread

**Preparation Time:** 3 hours 5 minutes

**Cooking Time:** 15 minutes

**Servings:** 10

**Difficulty:** Beginners

**Ingredients:**

- 1 cup buttermilk

- 1 egg

- 1/4 cup warm water (110 degrees F/45 degrees C)

- tablespoons honey

- 1 1/2 cups whole wheat flour

- 1 1/2 cups all-purpose flour

- 1/2 cup quick cooking oats

- tablespoons vegetable oil

- 1 1/2 teaspoons salt

- 1 1/2 teaspoons active dry yeast

**Directions:**

1. Check all ingredients and place them into the bread machine according to the manufacturer's suggestion.

2. Select Light Crust or Whole Wheat. Press Start.

**Nutrition:**

Calories: 200 calories;

Total Carbohydrate: 35 g

Cholesterol: 20 mg

Total Fat: 4.3 g

Protein: 6.6 g

Sodium: 384 mg

## 99. Sunflower & Flax Seed Bread

**Preparation Time:** 5 minutes

**Cooking Time:** 3 hours

**Servings:** 10 slices

**Difficulty:** Beginners

**Ingredients:**

- Water – 1 1/3 cups.

- Butter – 2 tablespoons.

- Honey – 3 tablespoons.

- Bread flour – 1 ½ cups.

- Whole wheat flour – 1 1/3 cups.

- Salt – 1 teaspoon.

- Active dry yeast – 1 teaspoon.

- Flax seeds – ½ cup.

- Sunflower seeds – ½ cup.

**Directions:**

1. Add all ingredients except for sunflower seeds into the bread machine pan.

2. Select basic setting then select light/medium crust and press start.

3. Add sunflower seeds just before the final kneading cycle.

4. Once loaf is done, remove the loaf pan from the machine. Allow it to cool for 10 minutes. Slice and serve.

Nutrition:

Calories 220,

Carbs 36.6g,

Fat 5.7g,

Protein 6.6g

## 100. Nutritious 9-Grain Bread

**Preparation Time:** 5 minutes

**Cooking Time:** 2 hours

**Servings:** 10 slices

**Difficulty:** Beginners

**Ingredients:**

- Warm water – 3/4 cup+2 tablespoons.

- Whole wheat flour – 1 cup.

- Bread flour – 1 cup.

- 9-grain cereal – ½ cup., crushed

- Salt – 1 teaspoon.

- Butter – 1 tablespoon.

- Sugar – 2 tablespoons.

- Milk powder – 1 tablespoon.

- Active dry yeast – 2 teaspoons.

**Directions:**

1.  Put all ingredients into the bread machine.

2.  Select whole wheat setting then select light/medium crust and start.

3.  Once loaf is done, remove the loaf pan from the machine.

4.  Allow it to cool for 10 minutes. Slice and serve.

Nutrition:

Calories 132,

Carbs 25g,

Fat 1.7g,

Protein 4.1g

## 101.  Oatmeal Sunflower Bread

**Preparation Time:** 15 minutes

**Cooking Time:** 3 hours 30 minutes

**Servings:** 10 slices

**Difficulty:** Beginners

**Ingredients:**

*   Water – 1 cup.

*   Honey – ¼ cup.

*   Butter – 2 tablespoons., softened

*   Bread flour – 3 cups.

*   Old fashioned oats – ½ cup.

*   Milk powder – 2 tablespoons.

- Salt – 1 ¼ teaspoons.

- Active dry yeast – 2 ¼ teaspoons.

- Sunflower seeds – ½ cup.

**Directions:**

1. Add all ingredients except for sunflower seeds into the bread machine pan.

2. Select basic setting then select light/medium crust and press start. Add sunflower seeds just before the final kneading cycle.

3. Once loaf is done, remove the loaf pan from the machine. Allow it to cool for 10 minutes. Slice and serve.

Nutrition:

Calories 215,

Carbs 39.3g,

Fat 4.2g,

Protein 5.4g

## 102.  Cornmeal Whole Wheat Bread

**Preparation Time:** 10 minutes

**Cooking Time:** 2 hours

**Servings:** 10 slices

**Difficulty:** Beginners

**Ingredients:**

- Active dry yeast – 2 ½ teaspoons.

- Water – 1 1/3 cups.

- Sugar – 2 tablespoons.

- Egg – 1, lightly beaten

- Butter – 2 tablespoons.

- Salt – 1 ½ teaspoons.

- Cornmeal – 3/4 cup.

- Whole wheat flour – 3/4 cup.

- Bread flour – 2 3/4 cups.

**Directions:**

1. Add all ingredients to the bread machine pan according to the bread machine manufacturer instructions.

2. Select basic bread setting then select medium crust and start. Once loaf is done, remove the loaf pan from the machine.

3. Allow it to cool for 10 minutes. Slice and serve.

Nutrition:

Calories 228,

Carbs 41.2g,

Fat 3.3g,

Protein 7.1g

## 103. Delicious Cranberry Bread

**Preparation Time:** 5 minutes

**Cooking Time:** 3 hours 27 minutes

**Servings:** 10 slices

**Difficulty:** Beginners

**Ingredients:**

- Warm water – 1 ½ cups
- Brown sugar – 2 tablespoons.
- Salt – 1 ½ teaspoons.
- Olive oil – 2 tablespoons.

- Flour – 4 cups

- Cinnamon – 1 ½ teaspoons.

- Cardamom – 1 ½ teaspoons.

- Dried cranberries – 1 cup

- Yeast – 2 teaspoons.

**Directions:**

1. Put all ingredients to the bread machine in the listed order.

2. Select sweet bread setting then select light/medium crust and start. Once loaf is done, remove the loaf pan from the machine.

3. Allow it to cool for 20 minutes. Slice and serve.

Nutrition:

Calories 223,

Carbs 41.9g,

Fat 3.3g,

Protein 5.5g

## 104. Coffee Raisin Bread

**Preparation Time:** 15 minutes

**Cooking Time:** 3 hours

**Servings:** 10 slices

**Difficulty:** Beginners

**Ingredients:**

- Active dry yeast – 2 ½ teaspoons.

- Ground cloves – ¼ teaspoon.

- Ground allspice – ¼ teaspoon.

- Ground cinnamon – 1 teaspoon.

- Sugar – 3 tablespoons.

- Egg – 1, lightly beaten

- Olive oil – 3 tablespoons.

- Strong brewed coffee – 1 cup.

- Bread flour – 3 cups.

- Raisins – 3/4 cup.

- Salt – 1 ½ teaspoons.

**Directions:**

1. Add all ingredients except for raisins into the bread machine pan.

2. Select basic setting then select light/medium crust and press start. Add raisins just before the final kneading cycle.

3. Once loaf is done, remove the loaf pan from the machine. Allow it to cool for 10 minutes. Slice and serve.

Nutrition:

Calories 230,

Carbs 41.5g,

Fat 5.1g,

Protein 5.2g

## 105.   Healthy Multigrain Bread

**Preparation Time:** 5 minutes

**Cooking Time:** 40 minutes

**Servings:** 10 slices

**Difficulty:** Beginners

**Ingredients:**

- Water – 1 ¼ cups.

- Butter – 2 tablespoons.

- Bread flour – 1 1/3 cups.

- Whole wheat flour – 1 ½ cups.

- Multigrain cereal – 1 cup.

- Brown sugar – 3 tablespoons.

- Salt – 1 ¼ teaspoons.

- Yeast – 2 ½ teaspoons.

## Directions:

1. Put ingredients listed into the bread machine pan. Select basic bread setting then select light/medium crust and start.

2. Once loaf is done, remove the loaf pan from the machine. Allow it to cool for 10 minutes. Slice and serve.

Nutrition:

Calories 159,

Carbs 29.3g,

Fat 2.9g,

Protein 4.6g

## 106.   Italian Pine Nut Bread

**Preparation Time:** 5 minutes

**Cooking Time:** 3 hours 30 minutes

**Servings:** 10 slices

**Difficulty:** Beginners

**Ingredients:**

- Water – 1 cup+ 2 tablespoons.

- Bread flour – 3 cups.

- Sugar – 2 tablespoons.

- Salt – 1 teaspoon.

- Active dry yeast – 1 1/4 teaspoons.

- Basil pesto – 1/3 cup.

- Flour – 2 tablespoons.

- Pine nuts – 1/3 cup.

**Directions:**

1. In a small container, combine basil pesto and flour and mix until well blended. Add pine nuts and stir well. Add water, bread flour, sugar, salt, and yeast into the bread machine pan.

2. Select basic setting then select medium crust and press start. Add basil pesto mixture just before the final kneading cycle.

3. Once loaf is done, remove the loaf pan from the machine. Allow it to cool for 10 minutes. Slice and serve.

Nutrition:

Calories 180,

Carbs 32.4g,

Fat 3.5g,

Protein 4.8g

## 107.  Whole Wheat Raisin Bread

**Preparation Time:** 5 minutes

**Cooking Time:** 2 hours

**Servings:** 10 slices

**Difficulty:** Beginners

**Ingredients:**

- Whole wheat flour – 3 ½ cups

- Dry yeast – 2 teaspoons.

- Eggs – 2, lightly beaten

- Butter – ¼ cup, softened

- Water – 3/4 cup

- Milk – 1/3 cup

- Salt – 1 teaspoon.

- Sugar – 1/3 cup

- Cinnamon – 4 teaspoons.

- Raisins – 1 cup

**Directions:**

1. Add water, milk, butter, and eggs to the bread pan. Add remaining ingredients except for yeast to the bread pan.

2. Make a small hole into the flour with your finger and add yeast to the hole. Make sure yeast will not be mixed with any liquids.

3. Select whole wheat setting then select light/medium crust and start. Once loaf is done, remove the loaf pan from the machine.

4. Allow it to cool for 10 minutes. Slice and serve.

Nutrition:

Calories 290,

Carbs 53.1g,

Fat 6.2g,

Protein 6.8g

## 108. Healthy Spelt Bread

**Preparation Time:** 15 minutes

**Cooking Time:** 40 minutes

**Servings:** 10 slices

**Difficulty:** Beginners

**Ingredients:**

- Milk – 1 ¼ cups.

- Sugar – 2 tablespoons.

- Olive oil – 2 tablespoons.

- Salt – 1 teaspoon.

- Spelt flour – 4 cups.

- Yeast – 2 ½ teaspoons.

**Directions:**

1. Add all ingredients according to the bread machine manufacturer instructions into the bread machine.

2. Select basic bread setting then select light/medium crust and start. Once loaf is done, remove the loaf pan from the machine.

3. Allow it to cool for 10 minutes. Slice and serve.

Nutrition:

Calories 223,

Carbs 40.3g,

Fat 4.5g,

Protein 9.2g

## 109. Awesome Rosemary Bread

**Preparation Time:** 5 minutes

**Cooking Time:** 2 hours

**Servings:** 8 slices

**Difficulty:** Beginners

**Ingredients:**

- 3/4 cup + 1 tablespoon water at 80 degrees F

- 1 2/3 tablespoons melted butter, cooled

- 2 teaspoons sugar

- 1 teaspoon salt

- 1 tablespoon fresh rosemary, chopped

- 2 cups white bread flour

- 1 1/3 teaspoons instant yeast

**Directions:**

1. Combine all of the ingredients to your bread machine, carefully following the instructions of the manufacturer.

2. Set the program of your bread machine to Basic/White Bread and set crust type to Medium.

3. Press START.

4. Wait until the cycle completes.

5. Once the loaf is ready, take the bucket out and allow the loaf to chill for 5 minutes.

6. Gently jiggle the bucket to take out the loaf.

Nutrition:

Total Carbs: 25g

Fiber: 1g

Protein: 4g

Fat: 3g

Calories: 142

# Chapter 11. Sourdough Breads

## 110. Garlic and Herb Flatbread Sourdough

**Preparation Time:** 1 hour

**Cooking Time:** 25- 30 minutes

**Servings:** 12

**Difficulty:** Expert

**Ingredients:**

- Dough

- 1 cup sourdough starter, fed or unfed

- 3/4 cup warm water

- teaspoons instant yeast

- cups all-purpose flour

- 1 1/2 teaspoons salt

- tablespoons olive oil

- Topping

- 1/2 teaspoon dried thyme

- 1/2 teaspoon dried oregano

- 1/2 teaspoon dried marjoram

- 1 teaspoon garlic powder

- 1/4 teaspoon onion powder

- 1/4 teaspoon salt

- 1/4 teaspoon pepper

- tablespoons olive oil

**Directions:**

1   Combine all the dough ingredients in the bowl of a stand mixer, and knead until smooth. Place in a lightly greased bowl and let rise for at least one hour. Punch down, then let rise again for at least one hour.

2   To prepare the topping, mix all ingredients except the olive oil in a small bowl.

3   Lightly grease a 9x13 baking pan or standard baking sheet, and pat and roll the dough into a long rectangle in the pan. Brush the olive oil over the dough, and sprinkle the herb and seasoning mixture over top. Cover and let rise for 15-20 minutes.

4   Preheat oven to 425F and bake for 25-30 minutes.

**Nutrition:**

Calories: 89 Cal

Fat: 3.7 g

Protein: 1.8 g


## 111.   Dinner Rolls

**Preparation Time:** 3 hours

**Cooking Time:** 5-10 minutes

**Servings:** 24 rolls

**Difficulty:** Expert

**Ingredients:**

- 1 cup sourdough starter

- 1 1/2 cups warm water

- 1 tablespoon yeast

- 1 tablespoon salt

- tablespoons sugar

- tablespoons olive oil

- cups all-purpose flour

- tablespoons butter, melted

**Directions:**

1  In a large bowl, mix the sourdough starter, water, yeast, salt, sugar, and oil. Add the flour, stirring until the mixture forms a dough. If needed, add more flour. Place the dough in a greased bowl, and let it rise until doubled in size, about 2 hours.

2  Remove the dough from the bowl, and divide it into 2-3 inch sized pieces. Place the buns into a greased 9x13 pan, and let them rise, covered, for about an hour.

3  Preheat oven to 350F, and bake the rolls for 15 minutes. Remove from the oven, brush with the melted butter, and bake for an additional 5-10 minutes.

**Nutrition:**

Calories: 128 Cal

Fat: 2.4 g

Protein: 3.2 g

Sugar: 1.1 g

## 112.  Sourdough Boule

**Preparation Time:** 4 hours

**Cooking Time:** 25-35 minutes

**Servings:** 12

**Difficulty:** Expert

## Ingredients:

- 275g Warm Water

- 500g sourdough starter

- 550g all-purpose flour

- 20g Salt

## Directions:

1  Combine the flour, warm water, and starter, and let sit, covered for at least 30 minutes.

2  After letting it sit, stir in the salt, and turn the dough out onto a floured surface. It will be quite sticky, but that's okay. Flatten the dough slightly (it's best to "slap" it onto the counter), then fold it in half a few times.

3  Cover the dough and let it rise. Repeat the slap and fold a few more times. Now cover the dough and let it rise for 2-4 hours.

4  When the dough at least doubles in size, gently pull it so the top of the dough is taught. Repeat several times. Let it rise for 2-4 hours once more.

5  Preheat to oven to 475F, and either place a baking stone or a cast iron pan in the oven to preheat. Place the risen dough on the stone or pot, and score the top in several spots. Bake for 20 minutes, then lower the heat to 425F, and bake for 25-35 minutes more. The boule will be golden brown.

## Nutrition:

Calories: 243 Cal

Fat: 0.7 g

Protein: 6.9 g

### 113.  Herbed Baguette

**Preparation Time:** 45 minutes

**Cooking Time:** 20-25 minutes

**Servings:** 12

**Difficulty:** Expert

**Ingredients:**

- 1 1/4 cups warm water
- cups sourdough starter, either fed or unfed
- to 5 cups all-purpose flour
- 1/2 teaspoons salt
- teaspoons sugar
- 1 tablespoon instant yeast
- 1 tablespoon fresh oregano, chopped
- 1 teaspoon fresh rosemary, chopped
- 1 tablespoon fresh basil, chopped
- any other desired herbs

**Directions:**

1  In the bowl of a stand mixer, combine all ingredients, knead with a dough hook (or use your hands) until smooth dough forms -- about 7 to 10 minutes, if needed, add more flour.

2  Place the dough in an oiled bowl, cover, and allow to rise for about 2 hours.

3  Punch down the dough, and divide it into 3 pieces. Shape each piece of dough into a baguette -- about 16 inches long. You can do this by rolling the dough into a log, folding it, rolling it into a log, then folding it and rolling it again.

4  Place the rolled baguette dough onto lined baking sheets, and cover. Let rise for one hour.

5   Preheat oven to 425F, and bake for 20-25 minutes

**Nutrition:**

Calories: 197 Cal

Fat: 0.6 g

Protein: 5.8 g

## 114.   Pumpernickel Bread

**Preparation Time:** 2 hours 10 minutes

**Cooking Time:** 50 minutes

**Servings:** 1 loaf

**Difficulty:** Expert

**Ingredients:**

- 1 1/8 cups warm water
- 1 ½ tablespoons vegetable oil
- 1/3 cup molasses
- tablespoons cocoa
- 1 tablespoon caraway seed (optional)
- 1 ½ teaspoon salt
- 1 ½ cups of bread flour
- 1 cup of rye flour
- 1 cup whole wheat flour
- 1 ½ tablespoons of vital wheat gluten (optional)
- ½ teaspoon of bread machine yeast

Directions:

1   Add all ingredients to bread machine pan.

2   Choose basic bread cycle.

3   Take bread out to cool and enjoy!

**Nutrition:**

Calories: 97 Cal

Fat: 1 g

Carbohydrates:19 g

Protein: 3 g

## 115.   Sauerkraut Rye

**Preparation Time:** 2 hours 20 minutes

**Cooking Time:** 50 minutes

**Servings:** 1 loaf

**Difficulty:** Expert

**Ingredients:**

- 1 cup sauerkraut, rinsed and drained

- ¾ cup warm water

- 1½ tablespoons molasses

- 1½ tablespoons butter

- 1½ tablespoons brown sugar

- 1 teaspoon caraway seeds

- 1½ teaspoons salt

- 1 cup rye flour

- cups bread flour

- 1½ teaspoons active dry yeast

**Directions:**

1  Add all of the ingredients to your bread machine.

2  Set the program of your bread machine to Basic/White Bread and set crust type to Medium

3  Press START

4  Wait until the cycle completes

5  Once the loaf is ready, take the bucket out and let the loaf cool for 5 minutes

6  Gently shake the bucket to remove the loaf

7  Transfer to a cooling rack, slice and serve

**Nutrition:**

Calories: 74 Cal

Fat: 2 g

Carbohydrates:12 g

Protein: 2 g

Fiber: 1 g

## 116.   Crusty Sourdough Bread

**Preparation Time:** 15 minutes ; 1 week (Starter)

**Cooking Time:** 3 hours

**Servings:** 1 loaf

**Difficulty:** Expert

**Ingredients:**

- 1/2 cup water
- cups bread flour
- tablespoons sugar
- 1 ½ teaspoon salt
- 1 teaspoon bread machine or quick active dry yeast

**Directions:**

1 Measure 1 cup of starter and remaining bread ingredients, add to bread machine pan.

2 Choose basic/white bread cycle with medium or light crust color.

**Nutrition:**

Calories: 165 calories;

Total Carbohydrate: 37 g

Total Fat: 0 g

Protein: 5 g

Sodium: 300 mg

Fiber: 1 g

## 117. Honey Sourdough Bread

**Preparation Time:** 15 minutes ; 1 week (Starter)

**Cooking Time:** 3 hours

**Servings:** 1 loaf

**Difficulty:** Beginners

## Ingredients:

- 2/3 cup sourdough starter
- 1/2 cup water
- 1 tablespoon vegetable oil
- tablespoons honey
- 1/2 teaspoon salt
- 1/2 cup high protein wheat flour
- cups bread flour
- 1 teaspoon active dry yeast

## Directions:

1. Measure 1 cup of starter and remaining bread ingredients, add to bread machine pan.

2. Choose basic/white bread cycle with medium or light crust color.

## Nutrition:

Calories: 175 calories;

Total Carbohydrate: 33 g

Total Fat: 0.3 g

Protein: 5.6 g

Sodium: 121 mg

Fiber: 1.9 g

## 118. Multigrain Sourdough Bread

**Preparation Time:** 15 minutes ; 1 week (Starter)

**Cooking Time:** 3 hours

**Servings:** 1 loaf

**Difficulty:** Beginners

**Ingredients:**

- cups sourdough starter
- tablespoons butter or 2 tablespoons olive oil
- 1/2 cup milk
- 1 teaspoon salt
- 1/4 cup honey
- 1/2 cup sunflower seeds
- 1/2 cup millet or 1/2 cup amaranth or 1/2 cup quinoa
- 1/2 cups multi-grain flour

**Directions:**

1  Add ingredients to bread machine pan.

2  Choose dough cycle.

3  Conventional Oven:

4  When cycle is complete, remove dough and place on lightly floured surface and shape into loaf.

5  Place in greased loaf pan, cover, and rise until bread is a couple inches above the edge.

6  Bake at 375 degrees for 40 to 50 minutes.

**Nutrition:**

Calories: 110 calories;

Total Carbohydrate: 13.5 g

Total Fat: 1.8 g

Protein: 2.7 g

Sodium: 213 mg

Fiber: 1.4 g

## 119.  Olive and Garlic Sourdough Bread

**Preparation Time:** 15 minutes ; 1 week (Starter)

**Cooking Time:** 3 hours

**Servings:** 1 loaf

**Difficulty:** Beginners

**Ingredients:**

- cups sourdough starter
- cups flour
- tablespoons olive oil
- tablespoons sugar
- teaspoon salt
- 1/2 cup chopped black olives
- cloves chopped garlic

**Directions:**

1   Add starter and bread ingredients to bread machine pan.

2   Choose dough cycle.

3   Conventional Oven:

4   Preheat oven to 350 degrees.

5   When cycle is complete, if dough is sticky add more flour.

6    Shape dough onto baking sheet or put into loaf pan

7    Bake for 35- 45 minutes until golden.

8    Cool before slicing.

**Nutrition:**

Calories: 150 calories;

Total Carbohydrate: 26.5 g

Total Fat: 0.5 g

Protein: 3.4 g

Sodium: 267 mg

Fiber: 1.1 g

## 120.    Czech Sourdough Bread

**Preparation Time:** 15 minutes ; 1 week (Starter)

**Cooking Time:** 3 hours

**Servings:** 1 loaf

**Difficulty:** Beginners

**Ingredients:**

- 1 cup non-dairy milk

- 1 tablespoon salt

- 1 tablespoon honey

- 1 cup sourdough starter

- 1 1/2 cups rye flour

- 1 cup bread flour

- 3/4 cup wheat flour

- 1/2 cup grated half-baked potato

- tablespoons wheat gluten

- teaspoons caraway seeds

## Directions:

1  Add ingredients to bread machine pan.

2  Choose the dough cycle.

3  The dough will need to rise, up to 24 hours, in the bread machine until doubles in size.

4  After rising, bake in bread machine for one hour.

## Nutrition:

Calories: 198 calories;

Total Carbohydrate: 39.9 g

Total Fat: 0.8 g

Protein: 6.5 g

Sodium: 888 mg

Fiber: 4.3 g

## 121.  French Sourdough Bread

**Preparation Time:** 15 minutes ; 1 week (Starter)

**Cooking Time:** 3 hours

**Servings:** 2 loaf

**Difficulty:** Beginners

**Ingredients:**

- cups sourdough starter

- 1 teaspoon salt

- 1/2 cup water

- cups white bread flour

- tablespoons white cornmeal

## Directions:

1  Add ingredients to bread machine pan, saving cornmeal for later.

2  Choose dough cycle.

3  Conventional Oven:

4  Preheat oven to 375 degrees.

5  At end of dough cycle, turn dough out onto a floured surface.

6  Add flour if dough is sticky.

7  Divide dough into 2 portions and flatten into an oval shape 1 ½ inch thick.

8  Fold ovals in half lengthwise and pinch seams to elongate.

9  Sprinkle cornmeal onto baking sheet and place the loaves seam side down.

10 Cover and let rise in until about doubled.

11 Place a shallow pan of hot water on the lower shelf of the oven;

12 Use a knife to make shallow, diagonal slashes in tops of loaves

13 Place the loaves in the oven and spray with fine water mister. Spray the oven walls as well.

14 Repeat spraying 3 times at one minute intervals.

15 Remove pan of water after 15 minutes of baking

16 Fully bake for 30 to 40 minutes or until golden brown.

## Nutrition:

Calories: 937 calories;

Total Carbohydrate: 196 g

Total Fat: 0.4 g

Protein: 26.5 g

Sodium: 1172 mg

Fiber: 7.3 g

## 122. Honey Sourdough Bread

**Preparation Time:** 15 minutes 1 week (Starter)

**Cooking Time:** 3 hours

**Servings:** 1 loaf

**Difficulty:** Beginners

**Ingredients:**

- 2/3 cup sourdough starter
- 1/2 cup water
- 1 tablespoon vegetable oil
- 2 tablespoons honey
- 1/2 teaspoon salt
- 1/2 cup high protein wheat flour
- 2 cups bread flour
- 1 teaspoon active dry yeast

**Directions:**

1. Measure 1 cup of starter and remaining bread ingredients, add to bread machine pan.

2. Choose basic/white bread cycle with medium or light crust color.

Nutrition:

Calories: 175 calories;

Total Carbohydrate: 33 g

Total Fat: 0.3 g

Protein: 5.6 g

Sodium: 121 mg

Fiber: 1.9 g

## 123. Multigrain Sourdough Bread

**Preparation Time:** 15 minutes; 1 week (Starter)

**Cooking Time:** 3 hours

**Servings:** 1 loaf

**Difficulty:** Beginners

**Ingredients:**

- 2 cups sourdough starter

- 2 tablespoons butter or 2 tablespoons olive oil

- 1/2 cup milk

- 1 teaspoon salt

- 1/4 cup honey

- 1/2 cup sunflower seeds

- 1/2 cup millet or 1/2 cup amaranth or 1/2 cup quinoa

- 3 1/2 cups multi-grain flour

**Directions:**

1. Add ingredients to bread machine pan.

2. Choose dough cycle.

3. Conventional Oven:

4. When cycle is over, take out dough and place on lightly floured surface and shape into loaf.

5. Place in greased loaf pan, cover, and rise until bread is a couple inches above the edge.

6. For 40 to 50 minutes, Bake at 375 degrees.

Nutrition:

Calories: 110 calories;

Total Carbohydrate: 13.5 g

Total Fat: 1.8 g

Protein: 2.7 g

Sodium: 213 mg

Fiber: 1.4 g

## 124. Olive and Garlic Sourdough Bread

**Preparation Time:** 15 minutes; 1 week (Starter)

**Cooking Time:** 3 hours

**Servings:** 1 loaf

**Difficulty:** Beginners

**Ingredients:**

- 2 cups sourdough starter

- 3 cups flour

- 2 tablespoons olive oil

- 2 tablespoons sugar

- 2 teaspoon salt

- 1/2 cup chopped black olives

- 6 cloves chopped garlic

**Directions:**

1. Add starter and bread ingredients to bread machine pan.

2. Choose dough cycle.

3. Conventional Oven:

4. Preheat oven to 350 degrees.

5. When cycle is complete, if dough is sticky add more flour.

6. Shape dough onto baking sheet or put into loaf pan

7. Bake for 35- 45 minutes until golden.

8. Cool before slicing.

Nutrition:

Calories: 150 calories;

Total Carbohydrate: 26.5 g

Total Fat: 0.5 g

Protein: 3.4 g

Sodium: 267 mg

Fiber: 1.1 g

## 125.  Sourdough Boule

**Preparation Time:** 4 hours

**Cooking Time:** 25-35 minutes

**Servings:** 12

**Difficulty:** Beginners

**Ingredients:**

- 275g Warm Water

- 500g sourdough starter

- 550g all-purpose flour

- 20g Salt

**Directions:**

1. Combine the flour, warm water, and starter, and let sit, covered for at least 30 minutes.

2. After letting it sit, stir in the salt, and turn the dough out onto a floured surface. It should be sticky, you do not have to worried.

3. Flatten the dough slightly (it's best to "slap" it onto the counter), then fold it in half a few times.

4. Cover the dough and let it rise. Repeat the slap and fold a few more times. Now cover the dough and let it rise for 2-4 hours.

5. When the dough at least doubles in size, gently pull it so the top of the dough is taught. Repeat several times. Let it rise for 2-4 hours once more.

6. Preheat to oven to 475F, and either place a baking stone or a cast iron pan in the oven to preheat.

7. Place the risen dough on the stone or pot, and score the top in several spots. For 20 minutes, bake then reduce the heat to 425F, and bake for 25-35 minutes more. The boule will be golden brown.

Nutrition:

Calories: 243 Cal

Fat: 0.7 g

Protein: 6.9 g

## 126. Herbed Baguette

**Preparation Time:** 45 minutes

**Cooking Time:** 20-25 minutes

**Servings:** 12

**Difficulty:** Beginners

**Ingredients:**

- 1 1/4 cups warm water
- 2 cups sourdough starter, either fed or unfed
- 4 to 5 cups all-purpose flour
- 2 1/2 teaspoons salt
- 2 teaspoons sugar
- 1 tablespoon instant yeast
- 1 tablespoon fresh oregano, chopped
- 1 teaspoon fresh rosemary, chopped
- 1 tablespoon fresh basil, chopped
- Any other desired herbs

**Directions:**

1. In the bowl of a mixer, combine all the ingredients, knead with a dough hook (or use your hands) until a smooth dough is formed - about 7 to 10 minutes, if necessary, add more flour.

2. Oil a bowl and place the dough, cover and let it rest for about 2 hours.

3. Beat the dough and divide it into 3 parts. Form each piece of dough into a loaf of bread, about 16 inches long. You can do this by rolling the dough into a trunk, folding it, rolling it into a trunk and then folding it again.

4. Place the rolled baguette dough onto lined baking sheets, and cover. Let rise for one hour.

5. Preheat oven to 425F, and bake for 20-25 minutes

Nutrition:

Calories: 197 Cal

Fat: 0.6 g

Protein: 5.8 g

## 127.   Czech Sourdough Bread

**Preparation Time:** 15 minutes; 1 week (Starter)

**Cooking Time:** 3 hours

**Servings:** 1 loaf

**Difficulty:** Beginners

**Ingredients:**

- 1 cup non-dairy milk

- 1 tablespoon salt

- 1 tablespoon honey

- 1 cup sourdough starter

- 1 1/2 cups rye flour

- 1 cup bread flour

- 3/4 cup wheat flour

- 1 1/2 cup grated half-baked potato

- 5 tablespoons wheat gluten

- 2 teaspoons caraway seeds

**Directions:**

1. Add ingredients to bread machine pan.

2. Choose the cycle of dough.

3. The dough should rise, up to 24 hours, in the bread machine until it doubles in size. After rising, bake in bread machine for one hour.

Nutrition:

Calories: 198 calories;

Total Carbohydrate: 39.9 g

Total Fat: 0.8 g

Protein: 6.5 g

Sodium: 888 mg

Fiber: 4.3 g

## 128.  Sauerkraut Rye

**Preparation Time:** 2 hours 20 minutes

**Cooking Time:** 50 minutes

**Servings:** 1 loaf

**Difficulty:** Beginners

**Ingredients:**

- 1 cup sauerkraut, rinsed and drained

- 3/4 cup warm water

- 1½ tablespoons molasses

- 1½ tablespoons butter

- 1½ tablespoons brown sugar

- 1 teaspoon caraway seeds

- 1½ teaspoons salt

- 1 cup rye flour

- 2 cups bread flour

- 1½ teaspoons active dry yeast

**Directions:**

1. Add all of the ingredients to your bread machine.

2. Set the program of your bread machine to Basic/White Bread and set crust type to Medium

3. Wait until the cycle completes

4. Once the loaf is ready, take the bucket out and let the loaf cool for 5 minutes

5. Gently shake the bucket to take out the loaf

Nutrition:

Calories: 74 Cal

Fat: 2 g

Carbohydrates: 12 g

Protein: 2 g

Fiber: 1 g

## 129.   French Sourdough Bread

**Preparation Time:** 15 minutes; 1 week (Starter)

**Cooking Time:** 3 hours

**Servings:** 2 loaf

**Difficulty:** Beginners

**Ingredients:**

- 2 cups sourdough starter

- 1 teaspoon salt

- 1/2 cup water

- 4 cups white bread flour

- 2 tablespoons white cornmeal

**Directions:**

1. Add ingredients to bread machine pan, saving cornmeal for later.

2. Choose dough cycle.

3. Conventional Oven:

4. Preheat oven to 375 degrees.

5. At end of dough cycle, place dough onto a surface that is floured.

6. Add flour if dough is sticky.

7. Divide dough into 2 portions and flatten into an oval shape 1 ½ inch thick.

8. Fold ovals in half lengthwise and pinch seams to elongate.

9. Sprinkle cornmeal onto baking sheet and place the loaves seam side down.

10. Cover and let rise in until about doubled.

11. Place a deep pan of hot water on the bottom shelf of the oven;

12. Use a knife to make shallow, diagonal slashes in tops of loaves

13. Place the loaves in the oven and sprinkle with fine water mister. Spray the oven walls as well.

14. Repeat spraying 3 times at one minute intervals.

15. Remove pan of water after 15 minutes of baking

16. Fully bake for 30 to 40 minutes or until golden brown.

Nutrition:

Calories: 937 calories;

Total Carbohydrate: 196 g

Total Fat: 0.4 g

Protein: 26.5 g

Sodium: 1172 mg

Fiber: 7.3 g

## 130. Sourdough Starter

**Preparation Time:** 5 days

**Cooking Time:**

**Servings:**

**Difficulty:** Beginners

**Ingredients:**

2 cups warm water

1 tablespoon sugar

1 active dry yeast

2 cups flour

1 proper container

1 spoon for stirring

**Directions:**

1.  Day 1:

2.  Combine the water, yeast, and sugar in a medium bowl, and whisk to combine. Gently stir in the flour until well combined, and transfer to your container. Let it sit, loosely covered, in a warm spot for 24 hours.

3.  Day 2 - 4

4.  Unlike the traditional starter, you don't need to feed this one yet. Stir it once or twice every 24 hours.

5.  Day 5:

6.  By now the starter should have developed the classic slightly sour smell. If not, don't worry; you just need to let it sit a bit longer. If it is ready, store it in the fridge, and feed it once a week until you're ready to use it. As with the traditional starter, you'll need to feed it the day before you plan to use it.

**Nutrition:**

Calories: 26 Cal

Fat: 0 g

Carbohydrates:6 g

Protein: 1 g

# Chapter 12. Breakfast & White Breads

### 131. Basic White Bread

**Preparation time:** 5 minutes

**Cooking time:** 3 hours

**Servings:** 16

**Difficulty:** Beginners

**Ingredients:**

- 1 cup warm water (about 110°F/45°C)

- 2 Tablespoon sugar

- 2¼ teaspoon (.25-ounce package) bread machine yeast

- ¼ cup rice bran oil

- 3 cups bread flour

- 1 teaspoon salt

**Directions:**

1. Add each ingredient to the bread machine in the order and at the temperature recommended by your bread machine manufacturer.

2. Close the lid, select the basic or white bread, low crust setting on your bread machine, and press start.

3. When the bread machine has finished baking, remove the bread and put it on a cooling rack.

Nutrition:

Carbs: 18 g

Fat: 1 g

Protein: 3 g

Calories: 95

## 132. Extra Buttery White Bread

**Preparation time:** 10 minutes

**Cooking time:** 3 hours 10 minutes

**Servings:** 16

**Difficulty:** Beginners

**Ingredients:**

- 1 1/8 cups milk

- 4 Tablespoon unsalted butter

- 3 cups bread flour

- 1½ Tablespoon white granulated sugar

- 1½ teaspoon salt

- 1½ teaspoon bread machine yeast

**Directions:**

1.  Soften the butter in your microwave.

2.  Add each ingredient to the bread machine in the order and at the temperature recommended by your bread machine manufacturer.

3.  Close the lid, select the basic or white bread, medium crust setting on your bread machine, and press start.

4.  When the bread machine has finished baking, remove the bread and put it on a cooling rack.

Nutrition:

Carbs: 22 g

Fat: 1 g

Protein: 4 g

Calories: 104

## 133. Mom's White Bread

**Preparation time:** 5 minutes

**Cooking time:** 3 hours

**Servings:** 16

**Difficulty:** Beginners

**Ingredients:**

- 1 cup and 3 Tablespoon water

- 2 Tablespoon vegetable oil

- 1½ teaspoon salt

- 2 Tablespoon sugar

- 3¼ cups white bread flour

- 2 teaspoon active dry yeast

**Directions:**

1. Add each ingredient to the bread machine in the order and at the temperature recommended by your bread machine manufacturer.

2. Close the lid, select the basic or white bread, medium crust setting on your bread machine, and press start.

3. When the bread machine has finished baking, remove the bread and put it on a cooling rack.

Nutrition:

Carbs: 1 g

Fat: 3 g

Protein: 90 g

Calories: 74

## 134. Vegan White Bread

**Preparation time:** 5 minutes

**Cooking time:** 3 hours

**Servings:** 14

**Difficulty:** Beginners

**Ingredients:**

- 1 1/3 cups water

- 1/3 cup plant milk (I use silk soy original)

- 1½ teaspoon salt

- 2 Tablespoon granulated sugar

- 2 Tablespoon vegetable oil

- 3½ cups all-purpose flour

- 1¾ teaspoon bread machine yeast

Directions:

1. Add each ingredient to the bread machine in the order and at the temperature recommended by your bread machine manufacturer.

2. Close the lid, select the basic or white bread, medium crust setting on your bread machine, and press start.

3. When the bread machine has finished baking, remove the bread and put it on a cooling rack.

Nutrition:

Carbs: 13 g

Fat: 2 g

Protein: 3 g

Calories: 80

## 135. Rice Flour Rice Bread

**Preparation time:** 10 minutes

**Cooking time:** 3 hours 15 minutes

**Servings:** 16

**Difficulty:** Beginners

**Ingredients:**

- 3 eggs

- 1½ cups water

- 3 Tablespoon vegetable oil

- 1 teaspoon apple cider vinegar

- 2¼ teaspoon active dry yeast

- 3¼ cups white rice flour

- 2½ teaspoon xanthan gum

- 1½ teaspoon salt

- ½ cup dry milk powder

- 3 Tablespoon white sugar

## Directions:

1. In a medium-size bowl, add the oil, water, eggs, and vinegar.

2. In a large dish, add the yeast, salt, xanthan gum, dry milk powder, rice flour, and sugar. Mix with a whisk until incorporated.

3. Add each ingredient to the bread machine in the order and at the temperature recommended by your bread machine manufacturer.

4. Close the lid, select the whole wheat, medium crust setting on your bread machine, and press start.

5. When the bread machine has finished baking, remove the bread and put it on a cooling rack.

Nutrition:

Carbs: 24 g

Fat: 1 g

Protein: 2 g

Calories: 95

### 136. Italian White Bread

**Preparation time:** 5 minutes

**Cooking time:** 3 hours

**Servings:** 14

**Difficulty:** Beginners

**Ingredients:**

- ¾ cup cold water
- 2 cups bread flour
- 1 Tablespoon sugar
- 1 teaspoon salt
- 1 Tablespoon olive oil

- 1 teaspoon active dry yeast

**Directions:**

1. Add each ingredient to the bread machine in the order and at the temperature recommended by your bread machine manufacturer.

2. Close the lid, select the Italian or basic bread, low crust setting on your bread machine, and press start.

3. When the bread machine has finished baking, remove the bread and put it on a cooling rack.

Nutrition:

Carbs: 11 g

Fat: 1 g

Protein: 2 g

Calories: 78

## 137.   Anadama White Bread

**Preparation time:** 5 minutes

**Cooking time:** 3 hours

**Servings:** 14

**Difficulty:** Beginners

**Ingredients:**

- 1 1/8 cups water (110°F/43°C)

- 1/3 cup molasses

- 1½ Tablespoon butter at room temperature

- 1 teaspoon salt

- 1/3 cup yellow cornmeal

- 3½ cups bread flour

- 2½ teaspoon bread machine yeast

**Directions:**

1. Add each ingredient to the bread machine in the order and at the temperature recommended by your bread machine manufacturer.

2. Close the lid, select the basic bread, low crust setting on your bread machine, and press start.

3. When the bread machine has finished baking, remove the bread and put it on a cooling rack.

Nutrition:

Carbs: 19 g

Fat: 1 g

Protein: 2 g

Calories: 76

## 138. Soft White Bread

**Preparation time:** 5 minutes

**Cooking time:** 3 hours

**Servings:** 14

**Difficulty:** Beginners

**Ingredients:**

- 2 cups water
- 4 teaspoon yeast
- 6 Tablespoon sugar
- ½ cup vegetable oil
- 2 teaspoon salt

- 3 cups strong white flour

**Directions:**

1. Add each ingredient to the bread machine in the order and at the temperature recommended by your bread machine manufacturer.

2. Close the lid, select the basic bread, low crust setting on your bread machine, and press start.

3. When the bread machine has finished baking, remove the bread and put it on a cooling rack.

Nutrition:

Carbs: 18 g

Fat: 1 g

Protein: 4 g

Calories: 74

## 139. English muffin Bread

**Preparation time:** 5 minutes

**Cooking time:** 3 hours 40 minutes

**Servings:** 14

**Difficulty:** Beginners

**Ingredients:**

- 1 teaspoon vinegar

- 1/4 to 1/3 cup water

- 1 cup lukewarm milk

- 2 Tablespoon butter or 2 Tablespoon vegetable oil

- 1½ teaspoon salt

- 1½ teaspoon sugar

- ½ teaspoon baking powder

- 3½ cups unbleached all-purpose flour

- 2 1/4 teaspoon instant yeast

## Directions:

1. Add each ingredient to the bread machine in the order and at the temperature recommended by your bread machine manufacturer.

2. Close the lid, select the basic bread, low crust setting on your bread machine, and press start.

3. When the bread machine has finished baking, remove the bread and put it on a cooling rack.

Nutrition:

Carbs: 13 g

Fat: 1 g

Protein: 2 g

Calories: 62

# 140. Cranberry Orange Breakfast Bread

**Preparation time:** 5 minutes

**Cooking time:** 3 hours 10 minutes

**Servings:** 14

**Difficulty:** Beginners

**Ingredients:**

- 1 1/8 cup orange juice

- 2 Tablespoon vegetable oil

- 2 Tablespoon honey

- 3 cups bread flour

- 1 Tablespoon dry milk powder

- ½ teaspoon ground cinnamon

- ½ teaspoon ground allspice

- 1 teaspoon salt

- 1 (.25 ounce) package active dry yeast

- 1 Tablespoon grated orange zest

- 1 cup sweetened dried cranberries

- 1/3 cup chopped walnuts

## Directions:

1. Add each ingredient to the bread machine in the order and at the temperature recommended by your bread machine manufacturer.

2. Close the lid, select the basic bread, low crust setting on your bread machine, and press start.

3. Add the cranberries and chopped walnuts 5 to 10 minutes before last kneading cycle ends.

4. When the bread machine has finished baking, remove the bread and put it on a cooling rack.

Nutrition:

Carbs: 29 g

Fat: 2 g

Protein: 9 g

Calories: 56

## 141.  Buttermilk Honey Bread

**Preparation time:** 5 minutes

**Cooking time:** 3 hours 45 minutes

**Servings:** 14

**Difficulty:** Beginners

**Ingredients:**

- ½ cup water

- ¾ cup buttermilk

- ¼ cup honey

- 3 Tablespoon butter, softened and cut into pieces

- 3 cups bread flour

- 1½ teaspoon salt

- 2¼ teaspoon yeast (or 1 package)

**Directions:**

1. Add each ingredient to the bread machine in the order and at the temperature recommended by your bread machine manufacturer.

2. Close the lid, select the basic bread, medium crust setting on your bread machine and press start.

3. When the bread machine has finished baking, remove the bread and put it on a cooling rack.

Nutrition:

Carbs: 19 g

Fat: 1 g

Protein: 2 g

Calories: 92

## 142. Whole Wheat Breakfast Bread

**Preparation time:** 5 minutes

**Cooking time:** 3 hours 45 minutes

**Servings:** 14

**Difficulty:** Beginners

**Ingredients:**

- 3 cups white whole wheat flour

- ½ teaspoon salt

- 1 cup water

- ½ cup coconut oil, liquified

- 4 Tablespoon honey

- 2½ teaspoon active dry yeast

## Directions:

1. Add each ingredient to the bread machine in the order and at the temperature recommended by your bread machine manufacturer.

2. Close the lid, select the basic bread, medium crust setting on your bread machine and press start.

3. When the bread machine has finished baking, remove the bread and put it on a cooling rack.

Nutrition:

Carbs: 11 g

Fat: 3 g

Protein: 1 g

Calories: 60

# 143. Cinnamon-Raisin Bread

**Preparation time:** 5 minutes

**Cooking time:** 3 hours

**Servings:** 4

**Difficulty:** Beginners

**Ingredients:**

- 1 cup water
- 2 Tablespoon butter, softened
- 3 cups Gold Medal Better for Bread flour
- 3 Tablespoon sugar
- 1½ teaspoon salt

- 1 teaspoon ground cinnamon

- 2½ teaspoon bread machine yeast

- ¾ cup raisins

**Directions:**

1. Add each ingredient except the raisins to the bread machine in the order and at the temperature recommended by your bread machine manufacturer.

2. Close the lid, select the sweet or basic bread, medium crust setting on your bread machine and press start.

3. Add raisins 10 minutes before the last kneading cycle ends.

4. When the bread machine has finished baking, remove the bread and put it on a cooling rack.

Nutrition:

Carbs: 38 g

Fat: 2 g

Protein: 4 g

Calories: 180

## 144.   Butter Bread Rolls

**Preparation time:** 50 minutes

**Cooking time**: 45 minutes

**Servings**: 24 rolls

**Difficulty:** Beginners

**Ingredients:**

- 1 cup warm milk

- 1/2 cup butter or 1/2 cup margarine, softened

- 1/4 cup sugar

- 2 eggs

- 1 1/2 teaspoons salt

- 4 cups bread flour

- 2 1/4 teaspoons active dry yeast

## Directions:

1   In bread machine pan, put all ingredients in order suggested by manufacturer.

2   Select dough setting.

3   When cycle is completed, turn dough onto a lightly floured surface.

4   Divide dough into 24 portions.

5   Shape dough into balls.

6   Place in a greased 13 inch by 9-inch baking pan.

7   Cover and let rise in a warm place for 30-45 minutes.

8   Bake at 350 degrees for 13-16 minutes or until golden brown.

Nutrition:

Carbs: 38 g

Fat: 2 g

Protein: 4 g

Calories: 180

## 145.   Cranberry & Golden Raisin Bread

**Preparation time:** 5 minutes

**Cooking time:** 3 hours

**Servings:** 14

**Difficulty:** Beginners

**Ingredients:**

- 1 1/3 cups water

- 4 Tablespoon sliced butter

- 3 cups flour

- 1 cup old fashioned oatmeal

- 1/3 cup brown sugar

- 1 teaspoon salt

- 4 Tablespoon dried cranberries

- 4 Tablespoon golden raisins

- 2 teaspoon bread machine yeast

## Directions:

1. Add each ingredient except cranberries and golden raisins to the bread machine one by one, according to the manufacturer's instructions.

2. Close the lid, select the sweet or basic bread, medium crust setting on your bread machine and press start.

3. Add the cranberries and golden raisins 5 to 10 minutes before the last kneading cycle ends.

4. When the bread machine has finished baking, remove the bread and put it on a cooling rack.

Nutrition:

Carbs: 33 g

Fat: 3 g

Protein: 4 g

Calories: 175

# Chapter 13.   Sweet Breads

### 146.   Brownie Bread

**Preparation Time:** 1 hour 15 minutes

**Cooking Time:** 50 minutes

**Servings:** 1 loaf

**Difficulty:** Intermediate

**Ingredients:**

- 1 egg

- 1 egg yolk

- 1 teaspoon Salt

- 1/2 cup boiling water

- 1/2 cup cocoa powder, unsweetened

- 1/2 cup warm water

- 1/2 teaspoon Active dry yeast

- tablespoon Vegetable oil

- teaspoon White sugar

- 2/3 cup white sugar

- cups bread flour

**Directions:**

1   Put the cocoa powder in a small bow. Pour boiling water and dissolve the cocoa powder.

2   Put the warm water, yeast and the 2 teaspoon White sugar in another bowl. Dissolve yeast and sugar. Let stand for about 10 minutes, or until the mix is creamy.

3   Place the cocoa mix, the yeast mix, the flour, the 2/3 cup white sugar, the salt, the vegetable, and the egg in the bread pan. Select basic bread cycle.

4   Press starts.

**Nutrition:**

Calories: 70 Cal

Fat: 3 g

Carbohydrates:10 g

Protein: 1 g

## 147.   Black Forest Bread

**Preparation Time:** 2 hour 15 minutes

**Cooking Time:** 50 minutes

**Servings:** 1 loaf

**Difficulty:** Intermediate

**Ingredients:**

- 1 1/8 cups Warm water
- 1/3 cup Molasses
- 1 1/2 tablespoons Canola oil
- 1 1/2 cups Bread flour
- 1 cup Rye flour
- 1 cup Whole wheat flour
- 1 1/2 teaspoons Salt
- tablespoons Cocoa powder

- 1 1/2 tablespoons Caraway seeds

- teaspoons Active dry yeast

## Directions:

1   Place all ingredients into your bread maker according to manufacture.

2   Select type to a light crust.

3   Press starts.

4   Remembering to check while starting to knead.

5   If mixture is too dry add tablespoon warm water at a time.

6   If mixture is too wet add flour again a little at a time.

7   Mixture should go into a ball form, and just soft and slightly sticky to the finger touch. This goes for all types of breads when kneading.

## Nutrition:

Calories: 240 Cal

Fat: 4 g

Carbohydrates:29 g

Protein: 22 g

## 148.   Sweet Almond Anise Bread

**Preparation Time:** 2 hours 20 minutes

**Cooking Time:** 50 minutes

**Servings:** 1 loaf

**Difficulty:** Intermediate

**Ingredients:**

- ¾ cup water

- ¼ cup butter

- ¼ cup sugar

- ½ teaspoon salt

- cups bread flour

- 1 teaspoon anise seed

- teaspoons active dry yeast

- ½ cup almonds, chopped

## Directions:

1  Add all of the ingredients to your bread machine, carefully following the instructions of the manufacturer

2  Set the program of your bread machine to Basic/White Bread and set crust type to Medium

3  Press START

4  Wait until the cycle completes

5  Once the loaf is ready, take the bucket out and let the loaf cool for 5 minutes

6  Gently shake the bucket to remove the loaf

7  Transfer to a cooling rack, slice and serve

Enjoy!

## Nutrition:

Calories: 87 Cal

Fat: 4 g

Carbohydrates:7 g

Protein: 3 g

Fiber: 1 g

## 149. Chocolate Ginger and Hazelnut Bread

**Preparation Time:** 2 hours 50 minutes

**Cooking Time:** 45 minutes

**Servings:** 2 loaves

**Difficulty:** Intermediate

**Ingredients:**

- 1/2 cup chopped hazelnuts

- teaspoon bread machine yeast

- 1/2 cups bread flour

- 1 teaspoon salt

- 1 1/2 tablespoon dry skim milk powder

- tablespoon light brown sugar

- tablespoon candied ginger, chopped

- 1/3 cup unsweetened coconut

- 1 1/2 tablespoon unsalted butter, cubed

- 1 cup, plus 2 tablespoon water, with a temperature of 80 to 90 degrees F (26 to 32 degrees C)

## Directions:

1   Put all the ingredients, except the hazelnuts, in the pan in this order: water, butter, coconut, candied ginger, brown sugar, milk, salt, flour, and yeast.

2   Secure the pan in the machine and close the lid. Put the toasted hazelnuts in the fruit and nut dispenser.

3   Turn the machine on. Select the basic setting and your desired color of the crust and press start.

4   Once done, carefully transfer the baked bread to a wire rack until cooled.

## Nutrition:

Calories: 273 calories;

Total Carbohydrate: 43 g

Total Fat: 11 g

Protein: 7 g

## 150.   White Chocolate Bread

**Preparation Time:** 3 hours

**Cooking Time:** 15 minutes

**Servings:** 12

**Difficulty:** Intermediate

## Ingredients:

- 1/4 cup warm water
- 1 cup warm milk
- 1 egg
- 1/4 cup butter, softened
- cups bread flour
- tablespoons brown sugar
- tablespoons white sugar
- 1 teaspoon salt
- 1 teaspoon ground cinnamon
- 1 (.25 oz.) package active dry yeast
- 1 cup white chocolate chips

## Directions:

1  Put all the ingredients together, except for the white chocolate chips, into the bread machine pan following the order suggested by the manufacturer.

2  Choose the cycle on the machine and press the Start button to run the machine.

3  Put in the white chocolate chips at the machine's signal if the machine used has a Fruit setting on it or you may put the white chocolate chips about 5 minutes before the kneading cycle ends.

## Nutrition:

Calories: 277 calories;

Total Carbohydrate: 39 g

Cholesterol: 30 mg

Total Fat: 10.5 g

Protein: 6.6 g

Sodium: 253 mg

## 151.   Cinnamon Raisin Bread

**Preparation Time:** 5 minutes

**Cooking Time:** 3 hours

**Servings:** 1 loaf

**Difficulty:** Intermediate

**Ingredients:**

- 1 cup water
- tablespoons margarine
- cups flour
- tablespoons sugar
- 1 1/2 teaspoons salt
- 1 teaspoon cinnamon
- 1/2 teaspoons yeast
- 3/4 cup raisins

**Directions:**

1  Add all the ingredients into pan except raisins.

2  Choose sweet bread setting.

3  When the machine beeps, add in raisins.

**Nutrition:**

Calories: 141 calories;

Total Carbohydrate: 26 g

Cholesterol: 00 mg

Total Fat: 2 g

Protein: 3.5 g

Sodium: 329 mg

Fiber: 1 g

## 152.   Chocolate Chip Bread

**Preparation Time:** 10 minutes

**Cooking Time:** 2 hours 50 minutes

**Servings:** 1 loaf

**Difficulty:** Intermediate

**Ingredients:**

- 1/4 cup water
- 1 cup milk
- 1 egg
- cups bread flour
- tablespoons brown sugar
- tablespoons white sugar
- 1 teaspoon salt
- 1 teaspoon ground cinnamon
- 1 1/2 teaspoon active dry yeast
- tablespoons margarine, softened

- 3/4 cup semisweet chocolate chips

**Directions:**

1  Add all the ingredients into pan except chocolate chips.

2  Choose mix bread

3  When the machine beeps, add in chips.

**Nutrition:**

Calories: 184 calories;

Total Carbohydrate: 30.6 g

Cholesterol: 14 mg

Total Fat: 5.2 g

Protein: 3.5 g

Sodium: 189 mg

Fiber: 1.3 g

## 153.   Peanut Butter Bread

**Preparation Time:** 10 minutes

**Cooking Time:** 3 hours

**Servings:** 1 loaf

**Difficulty:** Intermediate

**Ingredients:**

- 1 1/4 Cups water

- 1/2 cup Peanut butter - creamy or chunky

- 1 ½ cups whole wheat flour

- tablespoons Gluten flour

- 1 ½ cups bread flour

- 1/4 cup Brown sugar

- 1/2 teaspoon Salt -

- ¼ teaspoons Active dry yeast

**Directions:**

1   Add all the ingredients into pan.

2   Choose whole wheat bread setting, large loaf.

**Nutrition:**

Calories: 82 calories;

Total Carbohydrate: 13 g

Cholesterol: 13 mg

Total Fat: 2.2 g

Protein: 2.5 g

Sodium: 280 mg

Fiber: 1 g

## 154.   Hot Buttered Rum Bread

**Preparation Time:** 10 minutes

**Cooking Time:** 3 hours 40 minutes

**Servings:** 1 loaf

**Difficulty:** Intermediate

**Ingredients:**

- 1 egg
- 1 tablespoon rum extract
- tablespoons butter, softened
- cups bread flour

- tablespoons packed brown sugar

- 1 ¼ teaspoon salt

- 1/2 teaspoon ground cinnamon

- 1/4 teaspoon ground nutmeg

- 1/4 teaspoon ground cardamom

- 1 teaspoon bread machine or quick active dry yeast

- Topping:

- 1 egg yolk, beaten

- 1 ½ teaspoon finely chopped pecans

- 1 ½ teaspoon packed brown sugar

**Directions:**

1   Break egg into 1 cup, and add water to fil out measuring cup

2   Place egg mixture and bread ingredients into pan.

3   Choose basic bread setting and medium/light crust color.

4   While bread bakes, combine topping ingredients in small bowl, and brush on top of bread when there is 40 – 50 minutes remaining of the cook time.

**Nutrition:**

Calories: 170 calories;

Total Carbohydrate: 31 g

Cholesterol: 25 mg

Total Fat: 2.0 g

Protein: 4 g

Sodium: 270 mg

Fiber: 1 g

### 155.  Buttery Sweet Bread

**Preparation Time:** 10 minutes

**Cooking Time:** 3 hours 40 minutes

**Servings:** 1 loaf

**Difficulty:** Intermediate

**Ingredients:**

- 1-Pound Loaf
- 1/3 Cup Milk
- 1/4 Cup Water
- 1 Large Egg
- Tablespoons Butter or Margarine, Cut Up
- 3/4 Teaspoon Salt
- 2-1/4 Cups Bread Flour
- Tablespoons Sugar
- 1-1/2 Teaspoons Fleischmann's Bread Machine Yeast
- 1-1/2-Pound Loaf
- 1/2 Cup Milk
- 1/3 Cup Water
- 1 Large Egg
- 1/4 Cup Butter or Margarine, Cut Up
- 1 Teaspoon Salt

- 3-1/3 Cups Bread Flour

- 1/4 Cup Sugar

- Teaspoons Fleischmann's Bread

**Directions:**

1   Put ingredients into bread machine pan.

**Nutrition:**

Calories: 130 calories;

Total Carbohydrate: 17 g

Total Fat: 5 g

Protein: 3 g

## 156.   Almond and Chocolate Chip Bread

**Preparation Time:** 10 minutes

**Cooking Time:** 3 hours 40 minutes

**Servings:** 1 loaf

**Difficulty:** Intermediate

**Ingredients:**

- 1 cup plus 2 tablespoons water

- tablespoons butter or margarine, softened

- ½ teaspoon vanilla

- cups Gold Medal™ Better for Bread™ flour

- ¾ cup semisweet chocolate chips

- tablespoons sugar

- 1 tablespoon dry milk

- ¾ teaspoon salt

- 1 ½ teaspoons bread machine or quick active dry yeast

- 1/3 cup sliced almonds

**Directions:**

2   Measure and put all ingredients except almonds in bread machine pan. Add almonds at the Nut signal or 5 - 10 minutes before kneading cycle ends.

3   Select White cycle. Use Light crust color.

4   Take out baked bread from pan.

**Nutrition:**

Calories: 130 calories;

Total Carbohydrate: 18 g

Total Fat: 7 g

Protein: 1 g

Protein: 3 g

## 157. Sweet Pineapples Bread

**Preparation Time:** 2 hours

**Cooking Time:** 40 minutes

**Servings:** 5

**Difficulty:** Intermediate

**Ingredients:**

- oz dried pineapples

- oz raisins

- oz wheat flour

- eggs

- teaspoon baking powder

- oz brown sugar

- oz sugar

- Vanilla

## Directions:

1. Place the raisins into the warm water and leave for 20 minutes.

2. In a bowl, combine the sifted wheat flour, baking powder, brown sugar and vanilla.

3. Add the raisins and pineapples and mix well.

4. Whisk the eggs with the sugar until they have a smooth and creamy consistency.

5. Combine the eggs mixture with the flour and dried fruits mixture.

6. Pour the dough into the bread machine, close the lid and turn the bread machine on the basic/white bread program.

7. Bake the bread until the medium crust and after the bread is ready take it out and leave for 1 hour covered with the towel and only then you can slice the bread.

## Nutrition:

Calories: 144 calories;

Total Carbohydrate: 18 g

Total Fat: 9 g

Protein: 6 g

## 158.   Sweet Coconut Bread

**Preparation Time:** 2 hours

**Cooking Time:** 40 minutes

**Servings:** 6

**Difficulty:** Intermediate

**Ingredients:**

- oz shredded coconut
- oz walnuts, ground
- oz wheat flour
- oz coconut butter
- eggs
- teaspoon baking powder
- oz brown sugar
- Vanilla

**Directions:**

1   Whisk the eggs until they have a smooth and creamy consistency.

2   Combine the coconut butter with the brown sugar and vanilla and mix well, adding the eggs.

3   Combine the sifted wheat flour with the baking powder and eggs mixture and mix well until they have a smooth consistency.

4   Combine the dough with the shredded coconut and walnuts and then mix well.

5   Pour the dough into the bread machine, close the lid and turn the bread machine on the basic/white bread program.

6   Bake the bread until the medium crust and after the bread is ready take it out and leave for 1 hour covered with the towel and only then you can slice the bread.

**Nutrition:**

Calories: 164 calories;

Total Carbohydrate: 12 g

Total Fat: 8 g

Protein: 7 g

## 159.   Sweet Lemon Bread

**Preparation Time:** 3 hours

**Cooking Time:** 40 minutes

**Servings:** 6

**Difficulty:** Intermediate

**Ingredients:**

- oz lemon zest, minced

- oz of warm water (110-120 °F)

- 25 oz wheat flour

- teaspoon instant yeast

- tablespoon olive oil

- oz sugar

**Directions:**

1   Add the yeast and sugar into the warm water and melt them mixing in a bowl until smooth consistency.

2   After 20 minutes combine the yeast mixture with the olive oil and sifted wheat flour.

3   Combine the lemon zest with the dough, using a dough mixer, spiral mixer or food processor.

4   Spoon the dough into the bread machine and lubricate the surface of the dough with the water or the egg yolk.

5   Now close the lid and turn the bread machine on the basic/white bread program.

6   After the bread is ready take it out and leave for 1 hour covered with the towel and then you can eat the bread.

**Nutrition:**

Calories: 69 calories;

Total Carbohydrate: 6 g

Total Fat: 4 g

Protein: 3 g

## 160.   Brown & White Sugar Bread

**Preparation time:** 5 minutes

**Cooking time:** 2 hours 55 minutes

**Servings:** 12

**Difficulty:** Intermediate

Ingredients:

- 1 cup milk (room temperature)
- ¼ cup butter, softened
- 1 egg
- ¼ cup light brown sugar

- ¼ cup granulated white sugar

- 2 tablespoons ground cinnamon

- ¼ teaspoon salt

- 3 cups bread flour

- 2 teaspoons bread machine yeast

**Directions:**

1. Place all ingredients in the baking pan of the bread machine in the order recommended by the manufacturer.

2. Place the baking pan in the bread machine and close the lid.

3. Select Sweet Bread setting and then Medium Crust.

4. Press the start button.

5. Carefully, remove the baking pan from the machine and then invert the bread loaf onto a wire rack to cool completely before slicing.

6. With a sharp knife, cut bread loaf into desired-sized slices and serve.

Nutrition:

Calories 195

Total Fat 5 g

Saturated Fat 2.8 g

Cholesterol 25 mg

Sodium 94 mg

Total Carbs 33.2 g

Fiber 1.6 g

Sugar 8.2 g

Protein 4.7 g

## 161.   Molasses Bread

**Preparation time:** 5 minutes

**Cooking time:** 4 hours

**Servings:** 12

**Difficulty:** Intermediate

Ingredients:

- 1/3 cup milk
- ¼ cup water
- 3 tablespoons molasses
- 3 tablespoons butter, softened
- 2 cups bread flour
- 1¾ cups whole-wheat flour
- 2 tablespoons white sugar
- 1 teaspoon salt
- 2¼ teaspoons quick-rising yeast

**Directions:**

1. Place all ingredients in the baking pan of the bread machine in the order recommended by the manufacturer.

2. Place the baking pan in the bread machine and close the lid.

3. Select light browning setting.

4. Press the start button.

5. Carefully, remove the baking pan from the machine and then invert the bread loaf onto a wire rack to cool completely before slicing.

6. With a sharp knife, cut bread loaf into desired-sized slices and serve.

Nutrition:

Calories 205

Total Fat 3.9 g

Saturated Fat 1.9 g

Cholesterol 8 mg

Sodium 220 mg

Total Carbs 37.4 g

Fiber 3.1 g

Sugar 5.1 g

Protein 5.6 g

## 162.  Honey Bread

**Preparation time:** 5 minutes

**Cooking time:** 2 hours

**Servings:** 16

**Difficulty:** Intermediate

Ingredients:

- 1 cup plus 1 tablespoon milk

- 3 tablespoons honey

- 3 tablespoons butter, melted

- 3 cups bread flour

- 1½ teaspoons salt

- 2 teaspoons active dry yeast

**Directions:**

1.  Place all ingredients in the baking pan of the bread machine in the order recommended by the manufacturer.

2.  Place the baking pan in the bread machine and close the lid.

3.  Select White Bread setting and then Medium Crust.

4.  Press the start button.

5.  Carefully, remove the baking pan from the machine and then invert the bread loaf onto a wire rack to cool completely before slicing.

6.  With a sharp knife, cut bread loaf into desired-sized slices and serve.

Nutrition:

Calories 126

Total Fat 2.7 g

Saturated Fat 1.6 g

Cholesterol 70 mg

Sodium 241 mg

Total Carbs 22.1 g

Fiber 0.8 g

Sugar 4 g

Protein 3.2 g

## 163.  Maple Syrup Bread

**Preparation time:** 5 minutes

**Cooking time:** 3 hours

**Servings:** 12

**Difficulty:** Intermediate

**Ingredients:**

- 1 cup buttermilk

- 2 tablespoons maple syrup

- 2 tablespoons vegetable oil

- 2 tablespoons non-fat dry milk powder

- 1 cup whole-wheat flour

- 2 cups bread flour

- 1 teaspoon salt

- 1½ teaspoons bread machine yeast

**Directions:**

1. Place all ingredients in the baking pan of the bread machine in the order recommended by the manufacturer.

2. Place the baking pan in the bread machine and close the lid.

3. Select Basic setting.

4. Press the start button.

5. Carefully, remove the baking pan from the machine and then invert the bread loaf onto a wire rack to cool completely before slicing.

6. With a sharp knife, cut bread loaf into desired-sized slices and serve.

Nutrition:

Calories 151

Total Fat 2.6 g

Saturated Fat 0.6 g

Cholesterol 1 mg

Sodium 217 mg

Total Carbs 26.1 g

Fiber 0.4 g

Sugar 3.8 g

Protein 4.7 g

# 164. Peanut Butter & Jelly Bread

**Preparation time:** 5 minutes

**Cooking time:** 3 hours

**Servings:** 12

**Difficulty:** Intermediate

**Ingredients:**

- 1 cup water

- 1½ tablespoons vegetable oil

- ½ cup peanut butter

- ½ cup blackberry jelly

- 1 tablespoon white sugar

- 1 teaspoon salt

- 1 cup whole-wheat flour

- 2 cups bread flour
- 1½ teaspoons active dry yeast

**Directions:**

1. Place all ingredients in the baking pan of the bread machine in the order recommended by the manufacturer.

2. Place the baking pan in the bread machine and close the lid.

3. Select Sweet Bread setting.

4. Press the start button.

5. Carefully, remove the baking pan from the machine and then invert the bread loaf onto a wire rack to cool completely before slicing.

6. With a sharp knife, cut bread loaf into desired-sized slices and serve.

Nutrition:

Calories 218

Total Fat 7.2 g

Saturated Fat 1.5 g

Cholesterol 0 mg

Sodium 245 mg

Total Carbs 31.6 g

Fiber 1.1 g

Sugar 2.7 g

Protein 6.7 g

## 165.  Raisin Bread

**Preparation time:** 5 minutes

**Cooking time:** 3 hours

**Servings:** 12

**Difficulty:** Intermediate

**Ingredients:**

- 1 cup water
- 2 tablespoons margarine
- 3 cups bread flour
- 3 tablespoons white sugar
- 1 teaspoon salt
- 1 teaspoon ground cinnamon
- 2½ teaspoons active dry yeast
- ¾ cup golden raisins

## Directions:

1. Place all ingredients (except for raisins) in the baking pan of the bread machine in the order recommended by the manufacturer.

2. Place the baking pan in the bread machine and close the lid.

3. Select Sweet Bread setting.

4. Press the start button.

5. Wait for the bread machine to beep before adding the raisins.

6. Carefully, remove the baking pan from the machine and then invert the bread loaf onto a wire rack to cool completely before slicing.

7. With a sharp knife, cut bread loaf into desired-sized slices and serve.

Nutrition:

Calories 172

Total Fat 2.3 g

Saturated Fat 0.4 g

Cholesterol 0 mg

Sodium 218 mg

Total Carbs 34.5 g

Fiber 1.5 g

Sugar 8.4 g

Protein 3.9 g

## 166.  Currant Bread

**Preparation time:** 10 minutes

**Cooking time:** 3½ hours

**Servings:** 10

**Difficulty:** Intermediate

**Ingredients:**

- 1¼ cups warm milk

- 2 tablespoons light olive oil

- 2 tablespoons maple syrup

- 3 cups bread flour

- 2 teaspoons ground cardamom

- 1 teaspoon salt

- 2 teaspoons active dry yeast

- ½ cup currants

- ½ cup cashews, chopped finely

**Directions:**

1. Place all ingredients (except for currants and cashews) in the baking pan of the bread machine in the order recommended by the manufacturer.

2. Place the baking pan in the bread machine and close the lid.

3. Select Basic setting.

4. Press the start button.

5. Wait for the bread machine to beep before adding the currants and cashews.

6. Carefully, remove the baking pan from the machine and then invert the bread loaf onto a wire rack to cool completely before slicing.

7. With a sharp knife, cut bread loaf into desired-sized slices and serve.

Nutrition:

Calories 232

Total Fat 7.1 g

Saturated Fat 1.5 g

Cholesterol 3 mg

Sodium 250 mg

Total Carbs 36.4 g

Fiber 1.7 g

Sugar 4.6 g

Protein 6.4 g

## 167.  Pineapple Juice Bread

**Preparation time:** 5 minutes

**Cooking time:** 3 hours

**Servings:** 12

**Difficulty:** Intermediate

**Ingredients:**

- 3/4 cup fresh pineapple juice

- 1 egg

- 2 tablespoons vegetable oil

- 2 1/2 tablespoons honey

- 3/4 teaspoon salt

- 3 cups bread flour

- 2 tablespoons dry milk powder

- 2 teaspoons quick-rising yeast

**Directions:**

1. Place all ingredients in the baking pan of the bread machine in the order recommended by the manufacturer.

2. Place the baking pan in the bread machine and close the lid.

3. Select Sweet Bread setting and then Light Crust.

4. Press the start button.

5. Carefully, remove the baking pan from the machine and then invert the bread loaf onto a wire rack to cool completely before slicing.

6. With a sharp knife, cut bread loaf into desired-sized slices and serve.

Nutrition:

Calories 168

Total Fat 3 g

Saturated Fat 0.6 g

Cholesterol 14 mg

Sodium 161 mg

Total Carbs 30.5 g

Fiber 1 g

Sugar 5.9 g

Protein 4.5 g

# 168. Mocha Bread

**Preparation time:** 15 minutes

**Cooking time:** 2 hours 30 minutes

**Servings:** 12

**Difficulty:** Intermediate

**Ingredients:**

- 1/8 cup coffee-flavored liqueur
- ¼ cup water
- 1 (5-ounce) can evaporated milk
- 1 teaspoon salt
- 1½ teaspoons vegetable oil
- 3 cups bread flour
- 2 tablespoons brown sugar

- 1 teaspoon active dry yeast
- ¼ cup semi-sweet mini chocolate chips

**Directions:**

1. Put ingredients (except the chocolate chips) in the baking pan of the bread machine in the order recommended by the manufacturer.

2. Place the baking pan in the bread machine and close the lid.

3. Select Dough cycle.

4. Press the start button.

5. After the Dough cycle completes, remove the dough from the bread pan and place onto lightly floured surface.

6. With a plastic wrap, cover the dough for about 10 minutes.

7. Uncover the dough and roll it into a rectangle.

8. Sprinkle the dough with chocolate chips and then shape into a loaf.

9. Now, place the dough into greased loaf pan.

10. With a plastic wrap, cover the loaf pan and set in a warm place for 45 minutes or until doubled in size.

11. Preheat your oven to 375°F.

12. Bake for approximately 24–30 minutes or until a wooden skewer inserted in the center comes out clean.

13. Remove the loaf pan out of the oven and place onto a wire rack to cool for about 10 minutes.

14. Now, invert bread onto the wire rack to chill completely before slicing.

15. With a sharp knife, cut the bread loaf into desired-sized slices and serve.

Nutrition:

Calories 179

Total Fat 4.6 g

Saturated Fat 1.8 g

Cholesterol 3 mg

Sodium 208 mg

Total Carbs 29.8 g

Fiber 1.2 g

Sugar 5.3 g

Protein 4.2 g

# Chapter 14.  Holiday Bread

## 169.  Pumpkin Bread

**Preparation time:** 5 minutes

**Cooking time:** 1 hour

**Servings:** 14

**Difficulty:** Intermediate

**Ingredients:**

- ½ cup plus 2 tablespoons warm water

- ½ cup canned pumpkin puree

- ¼ cup butter, softened

- ¼ cup non-fat dry milk powder

- 2¾ cups bread flour

- ¼ cup brown sugar

- ¾ teaspoon salt

- 1 teaspoon ground cinnamon

- ½ teaspoon ground ginger

- 1/8 teaspoon ground nutmeg

- 2¼ teaspoons active dry yeast

## Directions:

1. Place all ingredients in the baking pan of the bread machine in the order recommended by the manufacturer.

2. Place the baking pan in the bread machine and close the lid.

3. Select Basic setting.

4. Press the start button.

5. Carefully, remove the baking pan from the machine and then invert the bread loaf onto a wire rack to cool completely before slicing.

6. With a sharp knife, cut bread loaf into desired-sized slices and serve.

Nutrition:

Calories 134

Total Fat 3.6 g

Saturated Fat 2.1 g

Cholesterol 9 mg

Sodium 149 mg

Total Carbs 22.4 g

Fiber 1.1 g

Sugar 2.9 g

Protein 2.9 g

## 170. Pumpkin Cranberry Bread

**Preparation time:** 10 minutes

**Cooking time:** 4 hours

**Servings:** 12

**Difficulty:** Intermediate

**Ingredients:**

- ¾ cup water
- 2/3 cup canned pumpkin
- 3 tablespoons brown sugar
- 2 tablespoons vegetable oil
- 2 cups all-purpose flour
- 1 cup whole-wheat flour
- 1¼ teaspoon salt

- ½ cup sweetened dried cranberries

- ½ cup walnuts, chopped

- 1¾ teaspoons active dry yeast

**Directions:**

1. Place all ingredients in the baking pan of the bread machine in the order recommended by the manufacturer.

2. Place the baking pan in the bread machine and close the lid.

3. Select Basic setting.

4. Press the start button.

5. Carefully, remove the baking pan from the machine and then invert the bread loaf onto a wire rack to cool completely before slicing.

6. With a sharp knife, cut bread loaf into desired-sized slices and serve.

Nutrition:

Calories 199

Total Fat 6 g

Saturated Fat 0.7 g

Cholesterol 0 mg

Sodium 247 mg

Total Carbs 31.4 g

Fiber 3.2 g

Sugar 5.1 g

Protein 5.6 g

## 171. Cranberry Bread

**Preparation time:** 10 minutes

**Cooking time:** 3 hours

**Servings:** 16

**Difficulty:** Intermediate

Ingredients:

1 cup plus 3 tablespoons water

¼ cup honey

2 tablespoons butter, softened

4 cups bread flour

1 teaspoon salt

2 teaspoons bread machine yeast

¾ cup dried cranberries

**Directions:**

1.  Place all ingredients (except the cranberries) in the baking pan of the bread machine in the order recommended by the manufacturer.

2.  Place the baking pan in the bread machine and close the lid.

3.  Select sweet bread setting.

4.  Press the start button.

5.  Wait for the bread machine to beep before adding the cranberries.

6.  Carefully, remove the baking pan from the machine and then invert the bread loaf onto a wire rack to cool completely before slicing.

7.  With a sharp knife, cut bread loaf into desired-sized slices and serve.

Nutrition:

Calories 147

Total Fat 1.8 g

Saturated Fat 1 g

Cholesterol 4 mg

Sodium 159 mg

Total Carbs 28.97 g

Fiber 1.2 g

Sugar 4.6 g

Protein 3.5 g

## 172. Cranberry Orange Bread

**Preparation time:** 10 minutes

**Cooking time:** 3 hours

**Servings:** 12

**Difficulty:** Intermediate

**Ingredients:**

- 3 cups all-purpose flour
- 1 cup dried cranberries
- ¾ cup plain yogurt
- ½ cup warm water
- 3 tablespoons honey
- 1 tablespoon butter, melted
- 2 teaspoons active dry yeast
- 1½ teaspoons salt
- 1 teaspoon orange oil

**Directions:**

1. Place all ingredients in the baking pan of the bread machine in the order recommended by the manufacturer.

2. Place the baking pan in the bread machine and close the lid.

3. Select Basic setting and then Light Crust.

4. Press the start button.

5. Carefully, remove the baking pan from the machine and then invert the bread loaf onto a wire rack to cool completely before slicing.

6. With a sharp knife, cut bread loaf into desired-sized slices and serve.

Nutrition:

Calories 166

Total Fat 2.7 g

Saturated Fat 1 g

Cholesterol 3 mg

Sodium 309 mg

Total Carbs 30.4 g

Fiber 1.3 g

Sugar 5.8 g

Protein 4.4 g

## 173. Orange Bread

**Preparation time:** 10 minutes

**Cooking time:** 3 hours

**Servings:** 12

**Difficulty:** Intermediate

**Ingredients:**

- 1¼ cups water
- 3 tablespoons powdered milk
- 1½ tablespoons vegetable oil
- 3 tablespoons honey
- 2½ cups bread flour
- ¾ cup amaranth flour
- 1/3 cup whole-wheat flour

- ¾ teaspoon salt

- 3 tablespoons fresh orange zest, grated finely

- 2¼ teaspoons active dry yeast

**Directions:**

1. Place all ingredients in the baking pan of the bread machine in the order recommended by the manufacturer.

2. Place the baking pan in the bread machine and close the lid.

3. Select Basic setting.

4. Press the start button.

5. Carefully, remove the baking pan from the machine and then invert the bread loaf onto a wire rack to cool completely before slicing.

6. With a sharp knife, cut bread loaf into desired-sized slices and serve.

Nutrition:

Calories 197

Total Fat 2.9 g

Saturated Fat 0.6 g

Cholesterol 0 mg

Sodium 162 mg

Total Carbs 36.9 g

Fiber 2.6 g

Sugar 5.6 g

Protein 6.1 g

## 174.   Banana Chocolate Chip Bread

**Preparation time:** 10 minutes

**Cooking time:** 1 hour 40 minutes

**Servings:** 16

**Difficulty:** Intermediate

Ingredients:

- ½ cup warm milk
- 2 eggs
- ½ cup butter, melted
- 1 teaspoon vanilla extract
- 3 medium ripe bananas, peeled and mashed
- 1 cup granulated white sugar
- 2 cups all-purpose flour
- ½ teaspoon salt
- 2 teaspoons baking powder
- 1 teaspoon baking soda
- ½ cup chocolate chips

**Directions:**

1. Add ingredients (except for cranberries) in the baking pan of the bread machine in the order recommended by the manufacturer.

2. Place the baking pan in the bread machine and close the lid.

3. Select Quick Bread setting.

4. Press the start button.

5. Wait for the bread machine to beep before adding the chocolate chips.

6. Carefully, remove the baking pan from the machine and then invert the bread loaf onto a wire rack to cool completely before slicing.

7. With a sharp knife, cut bread loaf into desired-sized slices and serve.

Nutrition:

Calories 215

Total Fat 8.2 g

Saturated Fat 5 g

Cholesterol 38 mg

Sodium 210 mg

Total Carbs 33.4 g

Fiber 1.2 g

Sugar 18.4 g

Protein 3.2 g

## 175. Sweet Potato Bread

**Preparation time:** 10 minutes

**Cooking time:** 3 hours

**Servings:** 16

**Difficulty:** Intermediate

**Ingredients:**

- ½ cup warm water
- 1 teaspoon pure vanilla extract

- 1 cup boiled sweet potato, peeled, and mashed

- 4 cups bread flour

- ½ teaspoon ground cinnamon

- 2 tablespoons butter, softened

- 1/3 cup brown sugar

- 1 teaspoon salt

- 2 teaspoons active dry yeast

- 2 tablespoons powdered milk

**Directions:**

1. Place all ingredients in the baking pan of the bread machine in the order recommended by the manufacturer.

2. Place the baking pan in the bread machine and close the lid.

3. Select White Bread setting.

4. Press the start button.

5. Carefully, remove the baking pan from the machine and then invert the bread loaf onto a wire rack to cool completely before slicing.

6. With a sharp knife, cut bread loaf into desired-sized slices and serve.

Nutrition:

Calories 155

Total Fat 1.8 g

Saturated Fat 1 g

Cholesterol 4 mg

Sodium 169 mg

Total Carbs 30.2 g

Fiber 1.4 g

Sugar 4.4 g

Protein 4.1 g

## 176.   Gingerbread

**Preparation time:** 10 minutes

**Cooking time:** 3 hours

**Servings:** 12

**Difficulty:** Intermediate

Ingredients:

- 3/4 cup milk

- 1/4 cup molasses

- 1 egg

- 3 tablespoons butter

- 3 1/3 cups bread flour

- 1 tablespoon brown sugar

- ¾ teaspoon salt

- ¾ teaspoon ground cinnamon

- ¾ teaspoon ground ginger

- 2¼ teaspoons active dry yeast

- 1/3 cup raisins

**Directions:**

1. Place all ingredients (except for raisins) in the baking pan of the bread machine in the order recommended by the manufacturer.

2. Place the baking pan in the bread machine and close the lid.

3. Select Basic setting and then Light Crust.

4. Press the start button.

5. Wait for the bread machine to beep before adding the raisins.

6. Carefully, remove the baking pan from the machine and then invert the bread loaf onto a wire rack to cool completely before slicing.

7. With a sharp knife, cut bread loaf into desired-sized slices and serve.

Nutrition:

Calories 202

Total Fat 4 g

Saturated Fat 2.2 g

Cholesterol 23 mg

Sodium 184 mg

Total Carbs 36.8 g

Fiber 1.3 g

Sugar 7.7 g

Protein 5 g

# 177. Raisin Cinnamon Swirl Bread

**Preparation time:** 15 minutes

**Cooking time:** 3 hours 35 minutes

**Servings:** 12

**Difficulty:** Intermediate

**Ingredients:**

**Dough**

- ¼ cup milk

- 1 large egg, beaten

- Water, as required

- ¼ cup butter, softened

- 1/3 cup white sugar

- 1 teaspoon salt

- 3½ cups bread flour

- 2 teaspoons active dry yeast

- ½ cup raisins

## Cinnamon Swirl

- 1/3 cup white sugar

- 3 teaspoons ground cinnamon

- 2 egg whites, beaten

- 1/3 cup butter, melted and cooled

## Directions:

1. For bread: Place milk and egg into a small bowl.

2. Add enough water to make 1 cup of mixture.

3. Place the egg mixture into the baking pan of the bread machine.

4. Place the remaining ingredients (except for raisins) on top in the order recommended by the manufacturer.

5. Place the baking pan in the bread machine and close the lid.

6. Select Dough cycle.

7. Press the start button.

8. Wait for the bread machine to beep before adding the raisins.

9. After Dough cycle completes, remove the dough from the bread pan and place onto lightly floured surface.

10. Roll the dough into a 10x12-inch rectangle.

11. For swirl: Mix together the sugar and cinnamon.

12. Brush the dough rectangle with 1 egg white, followed by the melted butter.

13. Now, sprinkle the dough with cinnamon sugar, leaving about a 1-inch border on each side.

14. From the short side, roll the dough and pinch the ends underneath.

15. Grease loaf pan and place the dough.

16. With a kitchen towel, cover the loaf pan and place in warm place for 1 hour or until doubled in size.

17. Preheat your oven to 350°F.

18. Brush the top of dough with remaining egg white.

19. Bake for approximately 35 minutes or until a wooden skewer inserted in the center comes out clean.

20. Remove the bread pan and place onto a wire rack to cool for about 15 minutes.

21. Cool bread before slicing

Nutrition:

Calories 297

Total Fat 10.6 g

Saturated Fat 6.3 g

Cholesterol 41 mg

Sodium 277 mg

Total Carbs 46.2 g

Fiber 1.7 g

Sugar 16.5 g

Protein 5.6 g

# 178.  Chocolate Chip Bread

**Preparation time:** 10 minutes

**Cooking time:** 2 hours 50 minutes

**Difficulty:** Intermediate

**Servings:** 12

**Ingredients:**

- 1 cup milk

- ¼ cup water

- 1 egg, beaten

- 2 tablespoons butter, softened

- 3 cups bread flour

- 2 tablespoons white sugar

- 1 teaspoon salt

- 1 teaspoon ground cinnamon

- 1½ teaspoons active dry yeast

- ¾ cup semi-sweet mini chocolate chips

## Directions:

1. Put ingredients (except the chocolate chips) in the baking pan of the bread machine in the order recommended by the manufacturer.

2. Place the baking pan in the bread machine and close the lid.

3. Select Mix Bread setting.

4. Press the start button.

5. Wait for the bread machine to beep before adding chocolate chips.

6. Carefully, remove the baking pan from the machine and then invert the bread loaf onto a wire rack to cool completely before slicing.

7. With a sharp knife, cut bread loaf into desired-sized slices and serve.

Nutrition:

Calories 226

Total Fat 7 g

Saturated Fat 4.1 g

Cholesterol 20 mg

Sodium 223 mg

Total Carbs 36.2 g

Fiber 1.8 g

Sugar 10 g

Protein 4.6 g

# Chapter 15.   Keto Bread

### 179.   Simple Keto Bread

Preparation Time: 35-40 minutes

Cooking Time: 0 minutes

Servings: 20 slices

Difficulty: Beginners

Ingredients:

- oz. almond flour

- oz. butter

- eggs

- 1 tbsp. of baking powder

- drops Stevia (optional)

- 1 pinch salt

Directions:

1   Preheat the oven at 375 degrees Fahrenheit.

2   Separate the whites of the eggs. Whisk them until peaks start forming.

3   Put the yolks of the eggs, one third portion of whisked egg whites, butter, baking powder, salt, and almond flour in one food processor and blend them. If you are using Stevia to balance the taste of eggs you can add that too. After blending, a thick lumpy dough will be formed.

4   Put the rest of the whisked egg whites. Blend once again. But do not over mix.

5   Pour the batter into one buttered eight-by-four loaf pan.

6   Keep it in the oven and bake for 30 minutes.

7   After it cools cut into 20 slices.

Nutrition:

Calories: 90

Fat: 7 grams

Carbohydrates: 2 grams

Fiber: 0.75 grams

Protein: 3 grams (Gaedke, n.d.)

## 180.   Paleo Bread

Preparation Time: 55 minutes

Cooking Time: 0 minutes

Servings: 12 slices

Difficulty: Beginners

Ingredients:

- 1 lb. almond flour
- eggs
- oz. ghee
- 1/8 tsp. salt
- 1 tsp. of baking powder

Directions:

1   Prepare the oven for baking by heating it to a temperature of 350 degrees Fahrenheit. Take some parchment paper and line one loaf pan.

2   Whisk the eggs for one minute at a high speed with a hand mixer. Add the ghee and whisk again.

3   Decrease the speed and mix the rest of the ingredients gradually to form a thick batter.

4   Put the batter in the baking pan. Spread it with one spatula.

5   Then bake for forty to 45 minutes until the top part becomes golden brown.

6   Place it on a cooling rack and allow it to cool for ten minutes. After that cut it into slices.

Nutrition:

Fat: 24 grams

Carbohydrates: 3 grams

Protein: 9 grams (Ashley, n.d.)

## 181.   Coconut Bread

Preparation Time: 40-50 minutes

Cooking Time: 0 minutes

Servings: 10 slices

Difficulty: Beginners

Ingredients:

- oz. coconut flour

- eggs

- oz. coconut oil

- oz. almond milk (unsweetened)

- 1/8 tbsp. salt

- 1/8 tbsp. of baking soda

Directions:

1   Preheat the oven at 350 degrees Fahrenheit.

2   Use parchment paper to line one eight-by-four inch loaf pan.

3   Combine salt, coconut flour and baking soda in one bowl.

4   Mix the oil, milk and eggs in a separate bowl.

5   Slowly mix the wet items with the dry items. Mix well to form a batter.

6   Dispense it into the loaf pan and bake for 40 to 50 minutes.

Nutrition:

Calories: 108

Fats: 8.7 grams

Carbohydrates: 3.4 grams

Fibers: 2.1 grams

Protein: 4.2 grams

Sugar: 0.5 grams

Sodium: 86 milligrams (Jess, n.d.)

## 182.   Bread with Macadamia Nuts

Preparation Time: 40 minutes

Cooking Time: 0 minutes

Servings: 10 slices

Difficulty: Beginners

Ingredients:

- 1/2 cup macadamia nuts

- eggs

- oz. coconut flour

- 1/2 tsp. vinegar (apple cider)

- 1/2 tsp. of baking soda

Directions:

1  Heat the oven beforehand to a temperature of 350 degrees Fahrenheit.

2  Place the nuts in a food processor. Pulse them until they form into nut butter. In case it is difficult to blend without liquid you can add the eggs, one by one, until the right consistency is reached.

3  Add the coconut flour, vinegar, and baking soda to it. Pulse until everything is combined properly.

4  Grease one baking pan and put the batter in it. Smoothen the surface of the batter with a spatula.

5  Move the pan on the oven's bottom rack and bake for 30 to forty minutes. By then the top part should become golden brown.

6  Move the pan out and let the bread cool in it for 15 to 20 minutes.

Nutrition:

1 Slice:

Calories: 151

Fat: 14 grams

Total carbohydrates: 4 grams

Net carbohydrates: 1 gram

Fiber: 3 grams

Protein: 5 grams (Deanna, 2018)

## 183. Zucchini Bread

Preparation Time: 1 hour 10 minutes

Cooking Time: 0 minutes

Servings: 16 slices

Difficulty: Beginners

Ingredients:

- 20 oz. almond flour

- oz. olive oil

- eggs

- 1 tsp. vanilla extract

- oz. erythritol

- 1/8 tbsp. nutmeg

- 1 tsp. cinnamon (ground)

- 1/4 tsp. ginger (ground)

- oz. zucchini (grated)

- oz. walnuts (chopped)

- 1/2 tsp. salt

- tsp. of baking powder

Directions:

2   Prepare the oven for baking and heat it to a temperature of 350 degrees Fahrenheit. Whisk the eggs, vanilla extract, and oil in one bowl. Keep them aside.

3   Mix almond flour, salt, nutmeg, ginger, cinnamon, baking powder, and erythritol in a separate bowl.

4   By means of a paper towel or cheesecloth, remove the extra water from zucchini. Then mix the zucchini with the whisked egg mixture.

5   After that, add the mixture of dry items into it. Blend with a hand mixer.

6   Spray some cooking spray on a nine-by-five loaf pan. Use a spoon to put the zucchini mixture into the pan.

7   Put the walnuts on it. Press them by a spatula so that they get embedded in the batter.

8   Bake for 60 to 70 minutes. By then the walnuts should have become slightly brown.

Nutrition:

1 Slice:

Calories: 200.13

Fat: 18.83 grams

Net carbohydrates: 2.6 grams

Protein: 5.59 grams (Keto Zucchini Bread with Walnuts, n.d.)

## 184.   Pumpkin Bread

Preparation Time: 50-55 minutes

Cooking Time: 0 minutes

Serving: 10 slices

Difficulty: Beginners

Ingredients:

- oz. butter

- oz. erythritol

- eggs

- oz. pumpkin puree

- 1/3 tbsp. vanilla extract

- oz. almond flour

- oz. coconut flour

- 1 clove

- 1/8 tbsp. salt

- 1/8 tbsp. nutmeg

- 1/8 tbsp. ginger

- 1/3 tbsp. cinnamon

- tsp. of baking powder

Directions:

1. Preheat oven to a temperature of 350 degrees Fahrenheit. Grease a nine-by-five loaf pan. Put a lining of parchment paper.

2. Take one big bowl and mix erythritol and butter until they become fluffy and light.

3. Put the eggs in it one by one. Mix well.

4. Add vanilla and pumpkin puree. Mix everything properly.

5. Take another bowl and mix coconut flour, almond flour, cinnamon, nutmeg, clove, ginger, salt, and baking powder. Break the lumps that may be there in the coconut or almond flours.

6. Then mix the dry items with the wet ones to form a batter.

7. Dispense it into the pan that you have prepared. Bake for 45 to 55 minutes.

Nutrition:

1 Slice:

Calories: 165

Carbohydrates: 6 grams

Fiber: 3 grams

Total fat: 14 grams

Fat (saturated): 7 grams

Cholesterol: 99 milligrams

Sodium: 76 milligrams

Sugar: 1 gram

Protein: 5 grams

## 185.   Low Carb Bread with Blueberries

Preparation Time: 55 minutes

Cooking Time: 0 minutes

Servings: 12 slices

Difficulty: Beginners

Ingredients:

- oz. almond butter

- oz. butter

- oz. almond flour

- oz. almond milk (without sugar)

- 1/8 tbsp. salt

- 2/3 tbsp. of baking powder

- eggs

- oz. blueberries

Directions:

1. Heat the oven at 350 degrees Fahrenheit.

2. Melt butter and almond butter in the microwave for 30 seconds. Stir to combine them.

3. Take a large bowl and whisk the almond flour, baking powder, and salt. Pour the melted butter and stir the mixture.

4. In one separate bowl, whisk the eggs and almond milk. Pour them into the almond flour mixture.

5. Add the blueberries to the batter.

6. Place a parchment paper on one loaf pan. Grease the paper lightly.

7. Put the batter in the pan. Bake for 45 minutes.

8. Before moving out from the pan, cool it for 30 minutes.

9. Cut the loaf and toast the slices before serving.

Nutrition:

Calories 156

Total fat 13 grams

Fat (saturated) 3 grams

Carbohydrates 4 grams

Fiber 1 gram

Sugar 1 gram

Protein 5 grams

Cholesterol 78 milligrams

Sodium 171 milligrams

Potassium 192 milligrams

Vitamin A 215IU

Calcium 106 milligrams

Iron 1 milligram

## 186.  Cinnamon Flavored Bread

Preparation Time: 35-40 minutes

Cooking Time: 0 minutes

Servings: 8 slices

Difficulty: Beginners

Ingredients:

- 1 lb. almond flour

- 1 oz. coconut flour

- oz. flaxseeds (ground)

- eggs

- 1/2 tbsp. vinegar (apple cider)

- 1/8 tbsp. salt

- 1/3 tbsp. of baking soda

- tbsp. honey

- tbsp. butter

- tsp. cinnamon

- 1/2 tsp. chia seeds

Directions:

1   Heat the oven beforehand to a temperature of 350 degrees Fahrenheit. Lay a piece of parchment paper on the bottom part of an eight-by-four bread pan and oil the sides of the pan.

2   Take a large bowl and mix coconut flour, almond flour, baking soda, ground flaxseeds, salt, and one and a half teaspoon cinnamon in it.

3   Whisk the eggs in another bowl. Then add honey, vinegar, and two tablespoons butter in it.

4   Mix the wet items into the dry ones and prepare the batter. Make sure that there are no bulges in the coconut or almond flours.

5   Dispense the batter into the greased pan and bake for 30 to 35 minutes. Take it out of the oven.

6   Whisk one tablespoon of butter and mix one and a half teaspoon of cinnamon in it. Brush this mixture on the bread.

7   Allow it to cool and then serve.

Nutrition:

Calories: 221

Total fats: 15.4 grams

Fat (saturated): 4.3 grams

Carbohydrates: 10.7 grams

Fiber: 3.1 grams

Sugar: 3.7 grams

Protein: 9.3 grams

Cholesterol: 103.3 milligrams

Sodium: 315.2 milligrams

Iron: 1.5 milligrams (Cotter, 2019)

## 187.   Best Keto Bread

Preparation Time: 10 minutes

Cooking time: 30 minutes

Servings: 20

Difficulty: Beginners

Ingredients:

- 1 ½ cup almond flour
- drops liquid stevia
- 1 pinch Pink Himalayan salt
- ¼ tsp. cream of tartar
- tsp. baking powder
- ¼ cup butter, melted
- large eggs, separated

Directions:

1  Preheat the oven to 375F.

2  To the egg whites, add cream of tartar and beat until soft peaks are formed.

3  Using a food processor, combine stevia, salt, baking powder, almond flour, melted butter, 1/3 of the beaten egg whites, and egg yolks. Mix well.

4  Then add the remaining 2/3 of the egg whites and gently process until fully mixed. Don't over mix.

5  Lubricate a (8 x 4) loaf pan and pour the mixture in it.

6  Bake for 30 minutes.

7  Enjoy.

Nutrition:

Calories: 90

Fat: 7g

Carb: 2g

Protein: 3g

## 188.   Bread De Soul

Preparation Time: 10 minutes

Cooking time: 45 minutes

Servings: 16

Difficulty: Beginners

Ingredients:

- ¼ tsp. cream of tartar
- ½ tsp. baking powder
- 1 tsp. xanthan gum
- 1/3 tsp. baking soda
- ½ tsp. salt
- 2/3 cup unflavored whey protein
- ¼ cup olive oil
- ¼ cup heavy whipping cream
- drops of sweet leaf stevia
- eggs
- ¼ cup butter
- oz. softened cream cheese

Directions:

1   Preheat the oven to 325F.

2   Using a bowl, microwave cream cheese and butter for 1 minute.

3   Remove and blend well with a hand mixer.

4   Add olive oil, eggs, heavy cream, and few drops of sweetener and blend well.

5   Blend the dry ingredients in another bowl.

6   Mix the wet ingredients with the dry ones and mix using a spoon. Don't use a hand blender to avoid whipping it too much.

7   Lubricate a bread pan and pour the mixture into the pan.

8   Bake in the oven until golden brown, about 45 minutes.

9   Cool and serve.

Nutrition:

Calories: 200

Fat: 15.2g

Carb: 1.8g

Protein: 10g

## 189.   Chia Seed Bread

Preparation Time: 10 minute

Cooking time: 40 minutes

Servings: 16 slices

Difficulty: Beginners

Ingredients:

- ½ tsp. xanthan gum

- ½ cup butter

- Tbsp. coconut oil

- 1 Tbsp. baking powder

- Tbsp. sesame seeds

- Tbsp. chia seeds

- ½ tsp. salt

- ¼ cup sunflower seeds

- cups almond flour

- eggs

Directions:

1. Preheat the oven to 350F.

2. Using a bowl, beat eggs on high for 1 to 2 minutes.

3. Beat in the xanthan gum and combine coconut oil and melted butter into eggs, beating continuously.

4. Set aside the sesame seeds, but add the rest of the ingredients.

5. Line a loaf pan with baking paper and place the mixture in it. Top the mixture with sesame seeds.

6. Bake for 35 to 40 minutes until a toothpick inserted comes out clean.

Nutrition:

Calories: 405

Fat: 37g

Carb: 4g

Protein: 14g

# 190.  Special Keto Bread

Preparation Time: 15 minutes

Cooking time: 40 minutes

Servings: 14

Difficulty: Beginners

Ingredients:

- tsp. baking powder
- ½ cup water
- 1 Tbsp. poppy seeds
- cups fine ground almond meal
- large eggs
- ½ cup olive oil
- ½ tsp. fine Himalayan salt

Directions:

1  Preheat the oven to 400F.

2  Using a bowl, combine salt, almond meal, and baking powder.

3  Drip in oil while mixing, until it forms a crumbly dough.

4  Make a little round hole in the middle of the dough and pour eggs into the middle of the dough.

5  Pour water and whisk eggs together with the mixer in the small circle until it is frothy.

6  Dispense batter into the prepared loaf pan and sprinkle poppy seeds on top.

7  Bake in the oven for 40 minutes in the center rack until firm and golden brown.

8  Cool in the oven for 30 minutes.

9   Slice and serve.

Nutrition:

Calories: 227

Fat: 21g

Carb: 4g

Protein: 7g

## 191.   Keto Fluffy Cloud Bread

Preparation Time: 25 minutes

Cooking time: 25 minutes

Servings: 3

Difficulty: Beginners

Ingredients:

- 1 pinch salt
- ½ Tbsp. ground psyllium husk powder
- ½ Tbsp. baking powder
- ¼ tsp. cream of tarter
- eggs, separated
- ½ cup, cream cheese

Directions:

1   Preheat the oven at 300F and line a baking tray with parchment paper.

2   Whisk egg whites using a bowl.

3   Mix egg yolks with cream cheese, salt, cream of tartar, psyllium husk powder, and baking powder in a bowl.

4   Fold in the egg whites carefully and transfer to the baking tray.

5   Place in the oven and bake for 25 minutes.

6   Remove from the oven and serve.

Nutrition:

Calories: 185

Fat: 16.4g

Carb: 3.9g

Protein: 6.6

## 192.   Splendid Low-Carb Bread

Preparation Time: 15 minutes

Cooking time: 60 to 70 minutes

Servings: 12

Difficulty: Beginners

Ingredients:

- ½ tsp. herbs, such as basil, rosemary, or oregano

- ½ tsp. garlic or onion powder

- 1 Tbsp. baking powder

- Tbsp. psyllium husk powder

- ½ cup almond flour

- ½ cup coconut flour

- ¼ tsp. salt

- 1 ½ cup egg whites

- Tbsp. oil or melted butter

- Tbsp. apple cider vinegar

- 1/3 to ¾ cup hot water

Directions:

1   Lubricate a loaf pan and preheat the oven at 350F.

2   Using a bowl, whisk the salt, psyllium husk powder, onion or garlic powder, coconut flour, almond flour, and baking powder.

3   Stir in egg whites, oil, and apple cider vinegar. Bit by bit add the hot water, stirring until dough increase in size. Do not add too much water.

4   Mold the dough into a rectangle and transfer to grease loaf pan.

5   Bake in the oven for 60 to 70 minutes, or until crust feels firm and brown on top.

6   Cool and serve.

Nutrition:

Calories: 97

Fat: 5.7g

Carb: 7.5g,

Protein: 4.1g

## 193.   Coconut Flour Almond Bread

Preparation Time: 10 minutes

Cooking time: 30 minutes

Servings: 4

Difficulty: Beginners

Ingredients:

- 1 Tbsp. butter, melted
- 1 Tbsp. coconut oil, melted
- eggs
- 1 tsp. baking soda
- Tbsp. ground flaxseed
- 1 ½ Tbsp. psyllium husk powder
- Tbsp. coconut flour
- 1 ½ cup almond flour

Directions:

1. Preheat the oven to 400F.
2. Mix the eggs in a bowl for a few minutes.
3. Add in the butter and coconut oil and mix once more for 1 minute.
4. Add the almond flour, coconut flour, baking soda, psyllium husk, and ground flaxseed to the mixture. Let sit for 15 minutes.
5. Lightly lubricate the loaf pan with coconut oil. Pour the mixture in the pan.
6. Place in the oven and bake until a toothpick inserted in it comes out dry, about 25 minutes.

Nutrition:

Calories: 475

Fat: 38g

Carb: 7g

Protein: 19g

## 194.   Quick Low-Carb Bread Loaf

Preparation Time: 45 minutes

Cooking time: 40 to 45 minutes

Servings: 16

Difficulty: Beginners

Ingredients:

- 2/3 cup coconut flour

- ½ cup butter, melted

- Tbsp. coconut oil, melted

- 1/3 cup almond flour

- ½ tsp. xanthan gum

- 1 tsp. baking powder

- large eggs

- ½ tsp. salt

Directions:

1   Preheat the oven to 350F. Cover the bread loaf pan with baking paper.

2   Beat the eggs until creamy.

3   Add in the coconut flour and almond flour, mixing them for 1 minute. Next, add the xanthan gum, coconut oil, baking powder, butter, and salt and mix them until the dough turns thick.

4   Put the completed dough into the prepared line of the bread loaf pan.

5　Set in the oven and bake for 40 to 45 minutes. Check with a knife.

6　Slice and serve.

Nutrition:

Calories: 174

Fat: 15g,

Carb: 5g

Protein: 5g

## 195.　Keto Bakers Bread

Preparation Time: 10 minutes

Cooking time: 20 minutes

Servings: 12

Difficulty: Beginners

Ingredients:

- Pinch of salt

- Tbsp. light cream cheese softened

- ½ tsp. cream of tartar

- eggs, yolks, and whites separated

Directions:

1　Heat 2 racks in the middle of the oven at 350F.

2　Line 2 baking pan with parchment paper, then grease with cooking spray.

3　Isolate egg whites from the egg yolks and place them in separate mixing bowls.

4 Beat the egg whites and cream of tartar with a hand mixer until stiff, about 3 to 5 minutes. Do not over-beat.

5 Whisk the cream cheese, salt, and egg yolks until smooth.

6 Slowly fold the cheese mix into the whites until fluffy.

7 Spoon ¼ cup measure of the batter onto the baking sheets, 6 mounds on each sheet.

8 Bake for 20 to 22 minutes, alternating racks halfway through.

9 Cool and serve.

Nutrition:

Calories: 41

Fat: 3.2g

Carb: 1g

Protein: 2.4g

## 196.  Almond Flour Lemon Bread

Preparation Time: 15 minutes

Cooking time: 45 minutes

Servings: 16

Difficulty: Beginners

Ingredients:

- 1 tsp. French herbs

- 1 tsp. lemon juice

- 1 tsp. salt

- 1 tsp. cream of tartar

- tsp. baking powder

- ¼ cup melted butter

- large eggs, divided

- ¼ cup coconut flour

- 1 ½ cup almond flour

Directions:

1  Preheat the oven to 350F.

2  Whip the cream of tartar and whites until soft peaks form.

3  Using a bowl, combine salt, egg yolks, melted butter, and lemon juice. Mix well.

4  Add coconut flour, almond flour, herbs, and baking powder. Mix well.

5  To the dough, add 1/3 the egg whites and mix until well-combined.

6  Add the remaining egg white's mixture and slowly mix to incorporate everything. Do not over mix.

7  Lubricate a loaf pan with butter or coconut oil.

8  Pour mixture into the loaf pan and bake for 30 minutes.

Nutrition:

Calories: 115

Fat: 9.9g

Carb: 3.3g

Protein: 5.2g

## 197.   Seed and Nut Bread

Preparation Time: 10 minutes

Cooking time: 40 minutes

Servings: 24

Difficulty: Beginners

Ingredients:

3 eggs

- ¼ cup avocado oil
- 1 tsp. psyllium husk powder
- 1 tsp. apple cider vinegar
- ¾ tsp. salt
- drops liquid stevia
- 1 ½ cups raw unsalted almonds
- ½ cup raw unsalted pepitas
- ½ cup raw unsalted sunflower seeds
- ½ cup flaxseeds

Directions:

1  Preheat the oven to 325F. Line a loaf pan with parchment paper.

2  In a giant bowl, whisk together the oil, eggs, psyllium husk powder, vinegar, salt, and liquid stevia.

3  Stir in the pepitas, almonds, sunflower seeds, and flaxseeds until well combined.

4  Dispense the batter into the prepared loaf pan, smooth it out and let it rest for 2 minutes.

5  Bake for 40 minutes.

6  Cool, slice, and serve.

Nutrition:

Calories: 131

Fat: 12g

Carb: 4g

Protein: 5g

## 198.   Blueberry Bread Loaf

Preparation Time: 20 minutes

Cooking time: 65 minutes

Servings: 12

Difficulty: Beginners

Ingredients:

- For the bread dough
- Tbsp. coconut flour
- Tbsp. melted butter
- 2/3 cup granulates swerve sweetener
- 1 ½ tsp. baking powder
- Tbsp. heavy whipping cream
- 1 ½ tsp. vanilla extract
- ½ tsp. cinnamon
- Tbsp. sour cream
- large eggs
- ½ tsp. salt
- ¾ cup blueberries

- For the topping

- 1 Tbsp. heavy whipping cream

- Tbsp. confectioner swerve sweetener

- 1 tsp. melted butter

- 1/8 tsp. vanilla extract

- ¼ tsp. lemon zest

Directions:

1   Preheat the oven at 350F and line a loaf pan with baking paper.

2   Using a bowl, mix granulated swerve, heavy whipping cream, eggs, and baking powder.

3   Once combined, add the butter, vanilla extract, salt, cinnamon, and sour cream. Then add the coconut flour to the batter.

4   Bake for 65 to 75 minutes.

5   Meanwhile, in a bowl, beat the vanilla extract, butter, heavy whipping cream, lemon zest, and confectioner swerve. Mix until creamy.

6   Cool the bread once baked. Then drizzle the icing topping on the bread.

7   Slice and serve.

**Nutrition:**

Calories: 155

Fat: 13g

Carb: 4g

Protein: 3g

## 199. Cloud Bread Loaf

Preparation time: 5 minutes

Cooking time: 50 minutes

Servings: 12

Difficulty: Beginners

Ingredients:

- 1/2 teaspoon baking powder
- 1/2 cup whey protein powder
- eggs separated
- 1/4 teaspoon salt
- 1/2 teaspoon cream of tartar
- 1/4 teaspoon onion powder
- ounces 170g sour cream
- 1/4 teaspoon garlic powder

Direction

1   Add all ingredients to the Bread Machine.

2   Select Dough setting and press Start. Mix the ingredients for about 4-5 minutes. After that press Stop button.

3   Smooth out the top of the loaf. Choose Bake mode and press Start. Let it bake for about 45 minutes.

4   Remove bread from the bread machine and let it rest for 10 minutes. Enjoy!

Nutrition:

84 calories

4.5 g fat

0.8 g total carb

7.5 g protein


## 200.   Bread with Psyllium

Preparation time: 5 minutes

Cooking time: 1 hour 30 minutes

Servings: 20

Difficulty: Beginners

Ingredients:

- 1 1/2 tablespoons baking powder

- ounces boiling water

- ounces almond flour

- ounces vinegar

- ounces Bob's Red Mill Golden Flax Meal

- ounces egg whites

- 100 grams Psyllium Husk Powder

- 1 teaspoon salt

Directions:

1   Add all ingredients to the Bread Machine.

2   Select Dough setting and press Start. Mix the ingredients for about 4-5 minutes. After that press Stop button.

3   Smooth out the top of the loaf. Choose Bake mode and press Start. Let it bake for about 1 hour 25 minutes.

4   Remove bread from the bread machine and let it rest for 10 minutes. Enjoy!

Nutrition:

127 calorie

9 g fat

10 g total carbs

5    g protein

## 201.   Multi-Purpose Bread Recipe

Preparation time: 5 minutes

Cooking time: 1 hour 15 minutes

Servings: 12

Difficulty: Beginners

Ingredients:

- 1/2 teaspoon herbs like rosemary, oregano or basil.

- 1/3-3/4 cup hot water

- cup coconut flour

- tablespoons apple cider vinegar

- 1/2 cup almond flour

- tablespoons oil/melted butter

- tablespoons psyllium husk powder

- 8-10 egg whites

- 1 tablespoon baking powder

- 1/4 teaspoon salt

- 1/2 teaspoon onion powder or garlic(optional)

Directions:

1   Add all ingredients to the Bread Machine.

2   Select Dough setting and press Start. Mix the ingredients for about 4-5 minutes. After that press Stop button.

3   Smooth out the top of the loaf. Choose Bake mode and press Start. Let it bake for about 1 hour 10 minutes.

4   Remove bread from the bread machine and let it rest for 10 minutes. Enjoy!

Nutrition:

97 calories

5.7 g fat

7.5 g total carbs

4.1 g protein

## 202.   Barbo's Dark Onion Rye Bread

Preparation time: 5 minutes

Cooking time: 35-45 minutes

Difficulty: Beginners

Servings: 16-18 thin slices

Ingredients:

- 1/4 cup water

- 1 tablespoon plus 1/4 teaspoon white vinegar

- 1/3 cups unblanched almond flour

- 1 teaspoon baking soda

- 1 tablespoon caraway seeds

- 1 tablespoon blackstrap molasses

- 1 teaspoon onion powder

- large eggs

- 1/4 teaspoon salt

- tablespoons oil

Directions:

1   To a food processor, add almond flour, caraway seeds, salt, onion powder and process for 50-60 seconds.

2   Add water, oil and process again for about 60 seconds.

3   Add all ingredients to the Bread Machine adding white vinegar and baking soda last.

4   Select Dough setting and press Start. Mix the ingredients for about 4-5 minutes. After that press Stop button.

5   Smooth out the top of the loaf. Choose Bake mode and press Start. Let it bake for about 50 minutes.

6   Remove bread from the bread machine and let it rest for 10 minutes. Enjoy!

Nutrition:

231 calories

20 g fat

7.5 g total carbs

8 g protein

# Chapter 16.   Dough Recipes

## 203.   Cheddar Biscuits

Preparation Time: 10 minutes

Cooking Time: 25 minutes

Difficulty: Beginners

Servings: 12

Ingredients:

- eggs
- ¼ cup unsalted butter, melted
- 1 ¼ cups, coconut milk
- ¼ tsp. salt
- ¼ tsp. baking soda
- ¼ tsp. garlic powder
- ½ cup finely shredded sharp cheddar cheese
- 1 Tbsp. fresh herb
- 2/3 cup coconut flour

Directions:

1   Preheat the oven to 350F. Grease a baking sheet.

2   Mix together the butter, eggs, milk, salt, baking soda, garlic powder, cheese, and herbs until well blended.

3   Add the coconut flour to the batter and mix until well blended. Let the batter sit then mix again.

4   Spoon about 2 tbsp. batter for each biscuit onto the greased baking sheet.

5   Bake for 25 minutes.

6   Serve warm.

Nutrition:

Calories: 125

Fat: 7g

Carb: 10g

Protein: 5g

## 204.   Savory Waffles

Preparation Time: 10 minutes

Cooking Time: 20 minutes

Servings: 4

Difficulty: Beginners

Ingredients:

- eggs
- 1 tsp. olive oil
- ½ cup sliced scallions
- ¾ cup grated pepper Jack cheese
- ¼ tsp. baking soda
- Pinch salt
- Tbsp. coconut flour

Directions:

1   Preheat the waffle iron to medium heat.

2   Mix all the ingredients using a bowl. Let the batter sit and mix once more.

3   Scoop ½ cup to 1-cup batter (depending on the size of the waffle iron) and pour onto the iron. Cook according to the manufacturer's directions.

4   Serve warm.

Nutrition:

Calories: 183

Fat: 13g

Carb: 4g

Protein: 12g

## 205.   Chocolate Chip Scones

Preparation Time: 10 minutes

Cooking Time: 10 minutes

Difficulty: Beginners

Servings: 8

Ingredients:

- cups almond flour
- 1 tsp. baking soda
- ¼ tsp. sea salt
- 1 egg
- Tbsp. low-carb sweetener
- Tbsp. milk, cream or yogurt

- ½ cup sugar-free chocolate chips

Directions:

1. Preheat the oven to 350F.

2. Using a bowl, add almond flour, baking soda, and salt and blend.

3. Then add the egg, sweetener, milk, and chocolate chips. Blend well.

4. Tap the dough into a ball and place it on parchment paper.

5. Roll the dough with a rolling pin into a large circle. Slice it into 8 triangular pieces.

6. Place the scones and parchment paper on a baking sheet and separate the scones about 1 inch or so apart.

7. For 7 to 10 minutes, bake until lightly browned.

8. Cool and serve.

Nutrition:

Calories: 213

Fat: 18g

Carb: 10g

Protein: 8g

## 206.  Snickerdoodles

Preparation Time: 10 minutes

Cooking Time: 10 minutes

Difficulty: Beginners

Servings: 20

Ingredients:

- cups almond flour

- Tbsp. coconut flour

- ¼ tsp. baking soda

- ¼ tsp. salt

- Tbsp. unsalted butter, melted

- 1/3 cup low-carb sweetener

- ¼ cup coconut milk

- 1 Tbsp. vanilla extract

- Tbsp. ground cinnamon

- Tbsp. low-carb granulated sweetener

Directions:

1  Preheat the oven to 350F.

2  Whisk the almond flour, coconut flour, salt and baking soda together using a bowl.

3  In another bowl, cream the butter, sweetener, milk and vanilla.

4  Put the flour mixture to the butter mixture and blend well.

5  Line baking sheets with parchment paper.

6  Blend the ground cinnamon and low-carb granulated sweetener together in a bowl. With your hands, roll a tbsp. of dough into a ball.

7  Reel the dough ball in the cinnamon mixture to fully coat.

8  Put the dough balls on the cookie sheet, spread about an inch apart, and flatten with the underside of a jar.

9  Bake for 8 to 10 minutes.

10  Cool and serve.

Nutrition:

Calories: 86

Fat: 7g

Carb: 3g

Protein: 3g

## 207.   No Corn Cornbread

Preparation Time: 10 minutes

Cooking Time: 20 minutes

Servings: 8

Difficulty: Beginners

Ingredients:

- ½ cup almond flour
- ¼ cup coconut flour
- ¼ tsp. salt
- ¼ tsp. baking soda
- eggs
- ¼ cup unsalted butter
- Tbsp. low-carb sweetener
- ½ cup coconut milk

Directions:

1   Preheat the oven to 325F.  Line a baking pan.

2   Combine dry ingredients in a bowl.

3   Put all the dry ingredients to the wet ones and blend well.

4  Dispense the batter into the baking pan and bake for 20 minutes.

5  Cool, slice, and serve.

Nutrition:

Calories: 65

Fat: 6g

Carb: 2g

Protein: 2g

## 208.  Garlic Cheese Bread Loaf

Preparation Time: 10 minutes

Cooking Time: 45 minutes

Servings: 10

Difficulty: Beginners

Ingredients:

- 1 Tbsp. parsley, chopped
- ½ cup butter, unsalted and softened
- Tbsp. garlic powder
- large eggs
- ½ tsp. oregano seasoning
- 1 tsp. baking powder
- cups almond flour
- ½ tsp. xanthan gum
- 1 cup cheddar cheese, shredded

- ½ tsp. salt

Directions:

1  Preheat the oven to 355F.

2  Line a baking pan with parchment paper.

3  In a food blender, pulse the eggs until smooth. Then combine the butter and pulse for 1 minute more.

4  Blend the almond flour and baking powder for 90 seconds or until thickens.

5  Finally, combine the garlic, oregano, parsley, and cheese until mixed.

6  Pour into the prepared and bake in the oven for 45 minutes.

7  Cool, slice, and serve.

Nutrition:

Calories: 299

Fat: 27g

Carb: 4g

Protein: 11g


## 209.  Iranian Flat Bread (Sangak)

Preparation Time: 3 hours

Cooking Time: 15 minutes

Servings: 6

Difficulty: Beginners

Ingredients:

- cups almond flour

- ½ cups warm water

- 1 Tbsp. instant yeast

- tsp. sesame seeds

- Salt to taste

Directions:

1  Add 1 tbsp. yeast to ½ cup warm water using a bowl and allow to stand for 5 minutes.

2  Add salt add 1 cup of water. Let stand for 10 minutes longer.

3  Put one cup of flour at a time, and then add the remaining water.

4  Knead the dough and then shape into a ball and let stand for 3 hours covered.

5  Preheat the oven to 480F.

6  By means of a rolling pin, roll out the dough, and divide into 6 balls.

7  Roll each ball into ½ inch thick rounds.

8  Place a parchment paper on the baking sheet and place the rolled rounds on it.

9  With a finger, make a small hole in the middle and add 2 tsp sesame seeds in each hole.

10  Bake for 3 to 4 minutes, then flip over and bake for 2 minutes more.

11  Serve.

Nutrition:

Calories: 26

Fat: 1g

Carb: 3.5g

Protein: 0.7g

## 210.   Puri Bread

Preparation Time: 10 minutes

Cooking Time: 5 minutes

Servings: 6

Difficulty: Beginners

Ingredients:

- 1 cup almond flour, sifted
- ½ cup of warm water
- Tbsp. clarified butter
- 1 cup olive oil for frying
- Salt to taste

Directions:

1   Salt the water and add the flour.

2   Build a hole in the center of the dough and pour warm clarified butter.

3   Knead the dough and let stand for 15 minutes, covered.

4   Shape into 6 balls.

5   Flatten the balls into 6 thin rounds using a rolling pin.

6   Heat enough oil to cover a round frying pan completely.

7   Place a puri in it when hot.

8   Fry for 20 seconds on each side.

9   Place on a paper towel.

10  Repeat with the rest of the puri and serve.

Nutrition:

Calories: 106

Fat: 3g

Carb: 6g

Protein: 3g

## 211. Pita Bread

Preparation Time: 10 minutes

Cooking Time: 15 minutes

Servings: 8

Difficulty: Beginners

Ingredients:

- cups almond flour, sifted
- ½ cup water
- Tbsp. olive oil
- Salt, to taste
- 1 tsp. black cumin

Directions:

1 Preheat the oven to 400F.

2 Combine the flour with salt. Add the water and olive oil.

3 Massage the dough and let stand for 15 minutes.

4 Shape the dough into 8 balls.

5 Put a parchment paper on the baking sheet and flatten the balls into 8 thin rounds.

6 Sprinkle black cumin.

7    Bake for 15 minutes, serve.

Nutrition:

Calories: 73

Fat: 6.9g

Carb: 1.6g

Protein: 1.6g

## 212.    Chocolate Zucchini Bread

Preparation Time: 10 minutes

Cooking Time: 20 minutes

Servings: 10

Difficulty: Beginners

Ingredients:

- cups grated zucchini, excess moisture removed
- eggs
- Tbsp. olive oil
- 1/3 cup low-carb sweetener
- 1 tsp. vanilla extract
- 1/3 cup coconut flour
- ¼ cup unsweetened cocoa powder
- ½ tsp. baking soda
- ½ tsp. salt
- 1/3 cup sugar-free chocolate chips

Directions:

1   Preheat the oven to 350F.

2   Grease the baking pan and line the entire pan with parchment paper.

3   In a food processor, blend the eggs, zucchini, oil, sweetener, and vanilla.

4   Add the flour, cocoa, baking soda, and salt to the zucchini mixture and stir until mixed. For a few seconds, let the batter sit.

5   Mix in the chocolate chips, then dispense the batter into the prepared pan.

6   Bake for 45 to 50 minutes.

7   Cool, slice, and serve.

Nutrition:

Calories: 149

Fat: 8g

Carb: 7g

Protein: 3g

## 213.   Cauliflower Breadsticks

Preparation Time: 10 minutes

Cooking Time: 35 minutes

Servings: 8

Difficulty: Beginners

Ingredients:

- cups riced cauliflower

- 1 cup mozzarella, shredded

- 1 tsp. Italian seasoning

- eggs

- ½ tsp. ground pepper

- 1 tsp. salt

- ½ tsp. granulated garlic

- ¼ cup Parmesan cheese as a topping

Directions:

1   Preheat the oven to 350F. Grease a baking sheet.

2   Beat the eggs until mixed well.

3   Combine riced cauliflower, mozzarella cheese, Italian seasoning, pepper, garlic, and salt and blend on low speed in a food processor. Combine with eggs.

4   Pour the dough into the prepared cookie sheet and pat the dough down to ¼ thick across the pan.

5   Bake for 30 minutes and dust the breadsticks with the parmesan cheese.

6   Put the breadsticks on the broil setting for 2 to 3 minutes, so the cheese melts.

7   Slice and serve.

Nutrition:

Calories: 165

Fat: 10g

Carb: 5g

Protein: 13g

## 214.  Cheddar Crackers

Preparation Time: 10 minutes

Cooking Time: 55 minutes

Servings: 8

Difficulty: Beginners

Ingredients:

- Tbsp. unsalted butter, softened slightly
- 1 egg white
- ¼ tsp. salt
- 1 cup plus 2 Tbsp. almond flour
- 1 tsp. minced fresh thyme
- 1 cup shredded sharp white cheddar cheese

Directions:

1   Preheat the oven to 300F.

2   Using a bowl, beat together the butter, egg white, and salt.

3   Stir in the almond flour, and thyme and then the cheddar until mixed.

4   Move the dough out between two pieces of parchment paper to a rectangle.

5   Peel off the top parchment paper and place the dough with the bottom parchment paper on a sheet pan.

6   Cut the dough into crackers with a pizza cutter.

7   Bake until golden, about 45 to 55 minutes, rotating the tray once halfway through.

8   Cool and serve.

Nutrition:

Calories: 200

Fat: 18g

Carb: 4g

Protein: 7g

## 215.   Sesame Almond Crackers

Preparation Time: 10 minutes

Cooking Time: 24 minutes

Servings: 8

Difficulty: Beginners

Ingredients:

- Tbsp. unsalted butter, softened slightly
- egg whites
- ½ tsp. salt
- ¼ tsp. black pepper
- ¼ cups almond flour
- Tbsp. sesame seeds

Directions:

1   Preheat the oven to 350F.

2   Using a bowl, beat the egg whites, butter, salt, and black pepper.

3   Stir in the almond flour and sesame seeds.

4   Move the dough out between two pieces of parchment paper to a rectangle.

5   Peel off the top parchment paper and place the dough on a sheet pan.

6   Cut the dough into crackers with a pizza cutter.

7   Bake for 18 to 24 minutes, or until golden, rotating the tray halfway through.

8   Serve.

Nutrition:

Calories: 299

Fat: 28g

Carb: 4g

Protein: 8g


## 216.   No-Yeast Sourdough Starter

Preparation Time: 10 minutes

Cooking Time: 0 minutes

Servings: 64

Difficulty: Beginners

Ingredients:

- cups all-purpose flour

- cups chlorine-free bottled water, at room temperature

Directions:

1   Stir together the flour and water in a large glass bowl with a wooden spoon.

2   With a plastic wrap, put a cover the bowl and place it in a warm area for 3 to 4 days, stirring at least twice a day, or until bubbly.

3   Store the starter in the refrigerator in a covered glass jar, and stir it before using.

4    Replenish your starter by adding back the same amount you removed, in equal parts flour and water.

Nutrition:

Calories: 14

Fat: 0g

Carbohydrates: 3g

Fiber: 0g

Protein: 0g

## 217.   Pizza Dough

**Preparation time:** 10 minutes

**Cooking time:** 1 hours 30 minutes

**Servings:** 2

**Difficulty:** Intermediate

**Ingredients:**

- 1 cup of warm water

- ¾ teaspoon salt

- 2 tablespoons olive oil

- 2 ½ cups flour

- 2 teaspoons sugar

- 2 teaspoons yeast

**Directions:**

1. Put ingredients in the bread maker.

2. Enable the Dough program and start the cycle.

3. Put the finished dough in a greased form or pan and distribute it. Allow standing for 10 minutes.

4. Preheat the oven to 400°F. On top of the dough, place the pizza sauce and the filling. Top with grated cheese.

5. For 15 to 20 minutes, bake till the edge is browned.

Nutrition:

Calories 716;

Total Fat 15.7g;

Saturated Fat 2.3g;

Cholesterol 0mg;

Sodium 881g;

Total Carbohydrate 124.8g;

Dietary Fiber 5.1g;

Total Sugars 4.4 g;

Protein 17.7g

## 218. Pizza Basis

**Preparation time:** 10 minutes

**Cooking time:** 1 hours 20 minutes

**Servings:** 2

**Difficulty:** Intermediate

**Ingredients:**

- 1 ¼ cups warm water

- 2 cups flour

- 1 cup Semolina flour

- ½ teaspoon sugar

- 1 teaspoon salt

- 1 teaspoon olive oil

- 2 teaspoons yeast

## Directions:

1. Place all the ingredients in the bread maker's bucket in the order recommended by the manufacturer. Select the Dough program.

2. After the dough has risen, use it as the base for the pizza.

Nutrition:

Calories 718;

Total Fat 4.4g;

Saturated Fat 0.6g;

Cholesterol 0mg;

Sodium 1173g;

Total Carbohydrate 145.6g;

Dietary Fiber 5.9g;

Total Sugars 1.5 g;

Protein 20.9g

## 219. Cinnamon Raisin Buns

**Preparation time:** 10 minutes

**Cooking time:** 45 minutes

**Servings:** 12

**Difficulty:** Intermediate

**Ingredients:**

For dough

- ½ cup milk
- ½ cup of water
- 2 tablespoons butter
- ¾ teaspoon salt
- 3 cups flour
- 2 ¼ teaspoon yeast
- 3 tablespoons sugar

- 1 egg

For filling

- 3 tablespoons butter, melted
- ¾ teaspoon ground cinnamon
- 1/3 cup sugar
- 1/3 cup raisins
- 1/3 cup chopped walnuts

For glaze

- 1 cup powdered sugar
- 1 ½ tablespoon melted butter
- ¼ teaspoon vanilla
- 1 ½ tablespoons milk

## Directions:

1. In a saucepan, heat ½ cup of milk, water, and 2 tablespoons of butter until they become hot.

2. Put the milk mixture, salt, flour, yeast, sugar, and eggs in the bread maker's bucket in the order recommended by the manufacturer. Select the Dough program. Click Start.

3. When through with the cycle, take out the dough from the bread maker. On a flour-covered surface, roll the dough into a large rectangle. Lubricate with softened butter.

4. Mix the cinnamon and sugar. Sprinkle the rectangle with the mixture. Generously sprinkle with raisins and/or chopped nuts.

5. Roll the dough into a roll, starting from the long side. Cut into 12 pieces. Put the buns slit-side down on a greased baking tray (25x35cm).

6. Cover and put in the heat until the dough almost doubles, about 30 minutes.

7. Preheat the oven to 375 degree F. Mix the powdered sugar, 1 1/2 tablespoon melted butter, vanilla, and 1 ½ tablespoon milk to get a thick frosting; set it aside.

8. Bake the buns in a preheated oven for 20 - 25 minutes, until browned. Remove and allow to cool down for 10 minutes. Frost the cooled buns with icing.

Nutrition:

Calories 308;

Total Fat 9.2g;

Saturated Fat 4.3g;

Cholesterol 31mg;

Sodium 202g;

Total Carbohydrate 53.2g;

Dietary Fiber 1.5g;

Total Sugars 27.9 g;

Protein 5.2g

## 220.  Italian Pie Calzone

**Preparation time:** 5 minutes

**Cooking time:** 1 hours 5 minutes

**Servings:** 12

**Difficulty:** Intermediate

**Ingredients:**

- 1 ¼ cups water

- 1 teaspoon salt

- 3 cups flour

- 1 teaspoon milk powder

- 1 ½ tablespoons sugar

- 2 teaspoons yeast

- ¾ cup tomato sauce for pizza

- 1 cup pepperoni sausage, finely chopped

- 1 ¼ cups grated mozzarella

- 2 tablespoons butter, melted

**Directions:**

1. Put water, salt, bread baking flour, soluble milk, sugar, and yeast in the bread maker's bucket in the order recommended by the manufacturer. Select the Dough setting.

2. After the end of the cycle, roll the dough on a lightly floured surface; form a rectangle measuring 45 x 25 cm. Transfer to a lightly oiled baking tray.

3. In a small bowl, combine the chopped pepperoni and mozzarella. Spoon the pizza sauce in a strip along the center of the dough. Add the filling of sausage and cheese.

4. Make diagonal incisions at a distance of 1 ½ cm from each other at the sides, receding 1 ½ cm from the filling.

5. Cross the strips on top of the filling, moistening it with the water. Lubricate with melted butter.

6. For 35 to 45 minutes bake at 360 degree F.

Nutrition:

Calories 247;

Total Fat 9.2g;

Saturated Fat 3.9g;

Cholesterol 22mg;

Sodium 590g;

Total Carbohydrate 32g;

Dietary Fiber 1.5g;

Total Sugars 2.8 g;

Protein 8.6g

## 221. French Baguettes

**Preparation time:** 20 minutes

**Cooking time:** 2 hours 30 minutes

**Servings:** 6

**Difficulty:** Intermediate

**Ingredients:**

- 1½ cups water

- 1½ teaspoons sugar

- 1½ teaspoons salt

- 3½ cups flour

- 1½ teaspoons yeast

- a mixture of different seeds (pumpkin, sunflower, black and white sesame)

**Directions:**

1. To prepare the dough for French baguettes in the bread maker, place all the ingredients in the bread maker's container in order: water, salt, and sugar, flour, yeast. Select the Yeast Dough program.

2. After 1½ hour, the dough for baguettes is ready.

3. Heat the oven to 440°F. Divide the dough into 2 parts. Lubricate the pan with oil. From the dough, form two French baguettes. Put on a baking pan and let it come for 10 minutes.

4. Then with a sharp knife, make shallow incisions on the surface of the baguettes. Sprinkle with water and sprinkle with a mixture of seeds. Leave it for another 10 minutes.

5. After the oven is warmed, put the pan with French baguettes in the oven for 5-7 minutes, then lower the heat to 360°F and bake for another 20-30 minutes until ready.

6. Transfer baguettes to a grate and cool.

7. Your crispy, delicious, fragrant French baguettes are ready… Bon Appetit!

Nutrition:

Calories 272;

Total Fat 0.8g;

Saturated Fat 0.1g;

Cholesterol 0mg;

Sodium 585g;

Total Carbohydrate 57g;

Dietary Fiber 2.2g;

Total Sugars 1.2g;

Protein 7.9g

# Chapter 17.    Buns & Bread

## 222.    Buns with Cottage Cheese

Preparation time: 10 minutes

Cooking time: 15 minutes

Servings: 8

Difficulty: Intermediate

Ingredients:

- eggs
- oz. Almond flour
- 1 oz. Erythritol
- 1/8 tsp. Stevia
- cinnamon and vanilla extract to taste Filling:
- ½ oz. Cottage cheese
- 1 egg
- cinnamon and vanilla extract to taste

Directions:

1   Prepare the filling by mixing its ingredients in a bowl.

2   Combine eggs with almond flour, blend until smooth. Add erythritol, stevia, and flavors to taste.

3   Spoon 1 tbsp. Dough into silicone cups. Spoon about 1 tsp. Filling on top, and bake at 365f for 15 minutes.

Nutrition:

Calories: 77

Fat: 5.2g

Carb: 6.7g

Protein: 5.8g

## 223.   Keto German Franks Bun

Preparation Time: 2 hours

Cooking Time: 9 minutes

Servings: 10

Difficulty: Intermediate

Ingredients:

- 1 ¼ cup almond milk, unsweetened, warmed
- ¼ cup sugar, granulated
- 1 small egg
- tbsps. butter
- ¾ tsp. salt
- ¾ cups almond flour
- 1 ¼ tsps. active dry yeast

Directions:

1   Position all ingredients in your bread machine pan in the order listed above.

2   Close the lid of your bread machine, select DOUGH cycle and press START.

3   Once cycle is finish, transfer the dough into a floured surface. Cut the dough in 10 slices long.

4    Flatten the dough into 5 x 4 inches. Then firmly roll the dough to form a cylindrical shape size of 5 x 1 inch.  Cover and let it rise for an hour or until the dough size doubles.

5    Preheat the oven at 350 degrees Fahrenheit. Arrange the dough in a greased baking sheet.

6    Place the baking sheet in the oven and bake for 9 minutes or until golden brown.

7    Cool then serve with your favorite franks.

Nutrition:

Calories: 16

Calories from fat: 87

Total Fat: 8 g

Total Carbohydrates: 3 g

Net Carbohydrates: 3 g

Protein: 6 g

## 224.    Keto Beer Bread

Preparation Time: 10 minutes

Cooking Time: 0

Servings: 10

Difficulty: Intermediate

Ingredients:

- oz. beer at room temperature

- oz. American cheese, shredded

- oz. Monterey Jack cheese, shredded

- 1 tbsp. sugar

- 1 ½ tsp. salt

- 1 tbsp. butter

- cups almond flour

tsp. active dry yeast

Directions:

1. Using a microwave, combine beer and American cheese and warm for 20 seconds.

2. Transfer the beer mixture on the bread machine pan and add all the other ingredients as listed above.

3. Close the bread machine lid and select WHITE BREAD setting (or BASIC setting and press START button.

4. When the cycle ends, cool the bread on a cooling rack.

Slice then serve with a bowl of chili or beef stew.

Nutrition:

Calories: 118

Calories from fat: 90

Total Fat: 9

Total Carbohydrates: 3 g

Net Carbohydrates: 3 g

Protein: 6 g

## 225. Keto Monterey Jack Jalapeno Bread

Preparation Time: 15 minutes

Cooking Time: 0

Servings: 12

Difficulty: Intermediate

Ingredients:

- 1 cup water
- tbsps. non-fat milk
- 1 ½ tbsps. sugar
- 1 ½ tsp. salt
- 1 ½ tbsps. butter, cubed
- ¼ cup Monterey Jack cheese, shredded
- 1 small jalapeno pepper
- cups almond flour
- tsp. active dry yeast

Directions:

1. Get rid of the seeds and stem of the jalapeno and mince finely.
2. Add the ingredients in the bread machine pan as listed above.
3. Close the lid and select BASIC cycle and light or medium CRUST COLOR, then press START.
4. Once the cycle ends, transfer the loaf in a cooling rack before slicing.
5. Serve as a side dish for salad or your favorite main course.

Nutrition:

Calories: 47

Calories from fat: 27

Total Fat: 3 g

Total Carbohydrates: 3 g

Net Carbohydrates: 2 g

Protein: 2 g

## 226. Keto Rye Sandwich Bread

Preparation Time: 10 minutes

Cooking Time: 3 hours

Servings: 12

Difficulty: Intermediate

Ingredients:

- ¼ cups warm water

- tbsps. melted butter, unsalted

- tsps. white sugar

- 1 ½ tsp. salt

- 1 tbsp. baking powder

- ¼ tsp. ground ginger

- ¼ cup granulated swerve

- cups vital wheat gluten

- cups super fine almond flour

- ¼ cup dark rye flour

tsps. active dry yeast

- 1 tbsp. caraway seeds

Directions:

367

1. Position all ingredients in the bread machine bucket and close the lid.

2. Select the WHOLE WHEAT cycle in your bread machine setting and choose light color on CRUST COLOR. Press START.

3. When the cycle ends, remove the pan from the bread machine and transfer the loaf on a cooling rack.

4. Slice and make a pastrami or Rueben sandwich to serve.

Nutrition:

Calories: 275

Calories from fat: 144

Total Fat: 16 g

Total Carbohydrates: 12

Net Carbohydrates: 8 g

Protein: 22 g

## 227.   Keto Orange Cranberry Bread

Preparation Time: 10 minutes

Cooking Time: 0

Servings  10

Difficulty: Intermediate

Ingredients:

- ¼ cup almond flour

- 1 tbsp. baking powder

- ¼ tsp. kosher salt

- large eggs

- 1 ½ cup buttermilk

- tbsp. canola oil

- 1 ½ cup brown sugar

- ½ tbsp. vanilla

- ½ tsp. nutmeg

- ¾ tsp. orange zest

- tbsp. orange juice, fresh

- 1 cup fresh cranberries, chopped

Directions:

1. Position all the ingredients in your bread machine bucket except for the cranberries.

2. Close the bread machine before selecting QUICK BREAD setting on your bread machine then press START.

3. Wait for the ping or the fruit and nut signal to open the lid and add the chopped cranberries. Cover the lid again and press START to continue.

4. When the cycle finishes, transfer the loaf to a wire rack and let it cool.

5. Slice and serve with your favorite salad.

Nutrition:

Calories: 141

Calories from fat: 110

Total Fat: 12 g

Total Carbohydrates: 5 g

Net Carbohydrates: 4 g

Protein: 4 g

## 228. Swiss Whole Meal Cheese Bread

Preparation time: 3 hours

Cooking Time: 0

Servings: 8

Difficulty: Intermediate

Ingredients:

- ¾ cup warm water

- 1 tablespoon sugar

- 1 teaspoon salt

- tablespoons green cheese

- 1 cup flour

- 9/10 cup flour whole-grain, finely ground

- 1 teaspoon yeast

- 1 teaspoon paprika

Directions:

1   Ingredients are listed in the order in which they are placed in the bread machine.

2   Add paprika at the signal.

3   The bread is gray, with a porous pulp. And, it does not become stale for a long time. It has a unique flavor, with very interesting cheese notes.

Nutrition:

Carbohydrates 5 g

Fats 1 g

Protein 4.1 g

Calories 118

## 229.   Mustard Beer Bread

Preparation time: 3 hours

Cooking Time: 0

Servings: 8

Difficulty: Intermediate

Ingredients:

- 1 ¼ cups dark beer

- 1/3 cups flour

- ¾ cup whole meal flour

- 1 tablespoon olive oil

- teaspoons mustard seeds

- 1 ½ teaspoons dry yeast

- 1 teaspoon salt

- teaspoons brown sugar

Directions:

1  Open a beer bottle and let it stand for 30 minutes to get out the gas.

2  In a bread maker's bucket, add the beer, mustard seeds, butter, sifted flour, and whole meal flour.

3  From different angles in the bucket, put salt and sugar. In the center of the flour, make a groove and fill with the mustard seeds.

4  Start the baking program.

Nutrition:

Carbohydrates 4.2 g

Fats 1 g

Protein 4.1 g

Calories 118

## 230.  Keto Flaxseed Honey Bread

Preparation Time: 10 minutes

Cooking Time: 20 minutes

Servings  18 slices

Difficulty: Intermediate

Ingredients:

- 1 cup warm water
- small eggs, lightly beaten
- ½ cup oat fiber
- 2/3 cup flaxseed meal
- 1.25 cup vital wheat gluten
- 1 tsp. salt
- tbsp. swerve powdered sweetener
- 1 tsp. honey
- ½ tsp. xanthan gum
- tbsps. Butter, unsalted
- 1 tbsp. dry active yeast

Directions:

1. Pour the water on the bread bucket. e
2. Add the eggs, honey, erythritol, salt, oat fiber, flaxseed meal, wheat gluten, and xanthan in this order. Add softened butter and yeast.
3. Place back the bread bucket in your bread machine and close the lid. Select BASIC then select medium darkness on CRUST COLOR. Press START button and wait until the bread cooks.
4. Cool bread on a cooling rack before slicing.
5. Serve with grilled chicken or any of your favorite grilled meat. Note that nutrition info is only for the bread.

Nutrition:

Calories: 96

Calories from fat: 36

Total Fat: 4 g

Total Carbohydrates: 5 g

Net Carbohydrates: 3 g

Protein: 8 g

## 231.   Basic Sweet Yeast Bread

Preparation time: 3 hours

Cooking Time: 0

Servings: 8

Difficulty: Beginners

Ingredients:

- 1 egg
- ¼ cup butter
- 1/3 cup sugar
- 1 cup milk
- ½ teaspoon salt
- cups almond flour
- 1 tablespoon active dry yeast
- After beeping:
- fruits/ground nuts

Directions:

1   Put all of the ingredients to your bread machine, carefully following the instructions of the manufacturer (except fruits/ground nuts).

2   Set the program of your bread machine to BASIC/SWEET and set crust type to LIGHT or MEDIUM.

3   Press START.

4   Once the machine beeps, add fruits/ground nuts.

5   Wait until the cycle completes.

6   Once the loaf is ready, take the bucket out and let the loaf cool for 5 minutes.

7   Gently shake the bucket to remove loaf.

8   Move it to a cooling rack, slice and serve.

9   Enjoy!

Nutrition:

Carbohydrates 2.7 g

Fats 7.6 g

Protein 8.8 g

Calories 338

## 232.   Apricot Prune Bread

Preparation time: 3 hours

Cooking Time: 0

Servings: 8

Difficulty: Beginners

Ingredients:

- 1 egg

- 4/5 cup whole milk

- ¼ cup apricot juice

- ¼ cup butter

- 1/5 cup sugar

- cups almond flour

- 1 tablespoon instant yeast

- ¼ teaspoon salt

- 5/8 cup prunes, chopped

- 5/8 cup dried apricots, chopped

Directions:

1. Put all of the ingredients to your bread machine, carefully following the instructions of the manufacturer (except apricots and prunes).

2. Set the program of your bread machine to BASIC/SWEET and set crust type to LIGHT or MEDIUM.

3. Press START.

4. Once the machine beeps, add apricots and prunes.

5. Wait until the cycle completes.

6. Once the loaf is ready, take the bucket out and let the loaf cool for 5 minutes.

7. Gently shake the bucket to remove loaf.

8. Move it to a cooling rack, slice and serve.

9. Enjoy!

Nutrition:

Carbohydrates 4 g

Fats 8.2 g

Protein 9 g

Calories 364

### 233. Gluten Free Chocolate Zucchini Bread

Preparation time: 5 minutes

Cooking Time: 0

Servings:  12

Difficulty: Beginners

Ingredients:

- 1 ½ cups coconut flour

- ¼ cup unsweetened cocoa powder

- ½ cup erythritol

- ½ tsp cinnamon

- 1 tsp baking soda

- 1 tsp baking powder

- ¼ tsp salt

- ¼ cup coconut oil, melted

- eggs

- 1 tsp vanilla

- cups zucchini, shredded

Directions:

1   Strip the zucchini and use paper towels to drain excess water, set aside.

2   Lightly beat eggs with coconut oil then add to bread machine pan.

3    Add the remaining ingredients to the pan.

4    Set bread machine to gluten free.

5    When the bread is done, remove bread machine pan from the bread machine.

6    Cool to some extent before transferring to a cooling rack.

7    You can store your bread for up to 5 days.

Nutrition:

Calories 185

Carbohydrates 6 g

Fats 17 g

Protein 5 g

## 234.   Not Your Everyday Bread

Preparation time: 7 minutes

Cooking Time: 0

Servings:  12

Difficulty: Beginners

Ingredients:

- tsp active dry yeast

- tbsp inulin

- ½ cup warm water

- ¾ cup almond flour

- ¼ cup golden flaxseed, ground

- tbsp whey protein isolate

- tbsp psyllium husk finely ground

- tsp xanthan gum

- tsp baking powder

- 1 tsp salt

- ¼ tsp cream of tartar

- ¼ tsp ginger, ground

- 1 egg

- egg whites

- tbsp ghee

- 1 tbsp apple cider vinegar

- ¼ cup sour cream

Directions:

1  Pour wet ingredients into bread machine pan.

2  Add dry ingredients, with the yeast on top.

3  Set bread machine to basic bread setting.

4  When the bread is done, remove bread machine pan from the bread machine.

5  Cool to some extent before transferring to a cooling rack.

6  You can store your bread for up to 5 days.

Nutrition:

Calories 175

Carbohydrates 6 g

Fats 14 g

Protein 5 g

# Chapter 18.   Bread Machine Recipes

### 235.   Great Plum Bread

Preparation time: 10 minutes

Cooking time: 50 minutes

Servings: 8

Difficulty: Beginners

Ingredients:

- 1 cup plums, pitted and chopped

- 1 and ½ cups coconut flour

- ¼ teaspoon baking soda

- ½ cup ghee, melted

- A pinch of salt

- 1 and ¼ cups swerve

- ½ teaspoon vanilla extract

- 1/3 cup coconut cream

- eggs, whisked

Directions:

1   Using a bowl, mix the flour with baking soda, salt, swerve, and the vanilla and stir.

2   Using a separate bowl, mix the plums with the remaining ingredients and stir.

3   Combine the 2 mixtures and stir the batter well.

4   Pour into 2 lined loaf pans and bake at temperature 350 degrees f for 50 minutes.

5   Cool the bread down, slice and serve them.

Nutrition:

calories 199

fat 8

fiber 3

carbs 6

protein 4

## 236.   Lime Bread

Preparation time: 10 minutes

Cooking time: 50 minutes

Servings: 8

Difficulty: Beginners

Ingredients:

- 2/3 cup ghee, melted
- cups swerve
- eggs, whisked
- teaspoons baking powder
- 1 cup almond milk
- tablespoons lime zest, grated
- tablespoons lime juice
- cups coconut flour
- Cooking spray

Directions:

1   Using a bowl, mix the flour with lime zest, baking powder and the swerve and stir.

2   In a separate bowl, mix the lime juice with the rest of the ingredients except the cooking spray and stir well.

3   Combine the 2 mixtures, stir the batter well and pour into 2 loaf pans greased with cooking spray and bake at 350 degrees f for 50 minutes.

4   Cool the bread down, slice and serve.

Nutrition:

calories 203

fat 7

fiber 3

carbs 4

protein 6

## 237.   Delicious Rhubarb Bread

Preparation time: 10 minutes

Cooking time: 40 minutes

Servings: 10

Difficulty: Beginners

Ingredients:

- 1 cup almond milk
- 1 teaspoon vanilla extract
- 1 tablespoon lemon juice
- 2/3 cup coconut oil, melted

- 1 egg

- 1 and ½ cups swerve

- an ½ cups coconut flour

- A pinch of salt

- cups rhubarb, chopped

- 1 teaspoon baking soda

- ½ teaspoon cinnamon powder

- 1 tablespoon ghee, melted

- Cooking spray

Directions:

1. Using a bowl, mix the vanilla with lemon juice, swerve, flour, salt, rhubarb, baking soda, and the cinnamon and stir.

2. Drop the rest of the ingredients except the cooking spray, stir the batter and pour into a loaf pan greased with cooking spray.

3. Bake at temperature 350 degrees f for 40 minutes, cool down, slice and serve.

Nutrition:

calories 200

fat 7

fiber 2

carbs 4

protein 6

## 238.  Delicious Cantaloupe Bread

Preparation time: 10 minutes

Cooking time: 1 hour

Servings: 8

Difficulty: Beginners

Ingredients:

- tablespoons stevia
- eggs
- 1 cup coconut oil, melted
- 1 tablespoon vanilla extract
- 1 teaspoon baking powder
- 1 teaspoon baking soda
- teaspoons cinnamon powder
- ½ teaspoon ginger, ground
- cups cantaloupe, peeled and pureed
- ½ cup ghee, melted
- cups almond flour

Directions:

1  Using a bowl, mix the flour with ginger, cinnamon, baking soda, baking powder, vanilla and the stevia and stir.

2  Drop the rest of the ingredients and stir the batter well.

3  Pour into 2 lined loaf pans and bake at 360 degrees f for 1 hour.

4  Cool the bread down, slice and serve.

Nutrition:

calories 211

fat 8

fiber 3

carbs 6

protein 6

## 239. Carrot Polenta Loaf

Preparation Time: 5 minutes

Cooking Time: 3 hours

Servings: 1 loaf

Difficulty: Beginners

Ingredients:

- oz. lukewarm water
- tablespoons extra-virgin olive oil
- 1 tsp salt
- 1 ½ tablespoons sugar
- 1 ½ tablespoons dried thyme
- 1 ½ cups freshly-grated carrots
- 1/2 cup yellow cornmeal
- 1 cup light rye flour
- ½ cups bread flour
- tsp instant active dry yeast

Directions

1   Add all ingredients to machine pan.

2   Select dough setting.

3   When cycle is complete, turn dough onto lightly floured surface.

4   Knead the dough and shape into an oval; cover with plastic wrap and let rest for 10 to 15 minutes.

5   After resting, turn bottom side up and flatten.

6   Make a fold at the top 1/3 of the way to the bottom. Then fold the bottom a 1/3 of the way over the top.

7   Preheat oven 400.

8   Dust a baking sheet with cornmeal, place dough on and cover in a warm place to rise for 20 minutes.

9   After rising, make 3 deep diagonal slashes on the top and brush the top of the bread with cold water.

10  Bake until nicely browned for approximately 20 to 25 minutes.

Nutrition:

146 Calories

1 mg cholesterol

3 g total fat

186 sodium

27 carb. 2 fiber

3,9 g protein

## 240. Wild Rice Cranberry Bread

Preparation Time: 5 minutes

Cooking Time: 3 hours

Servings: 1 loaf

Difficulty: Beginners

Ingredients:

- 1 ¼ cup water
- 1/4 cup skim milk powder
- 1 ¼ tsp salt
- tablespoon liquid honey
- 1 tablespoon extra-virgin olive oil
- cup all-purpose flour
- 3/4 cup cooked wild rice
- 1/4 cup pine nuts
- 3/4 tsp celery seeds
- 1/8 tsp freshly ground black pepper
- 1 tsp bread machine or instant yeast
- 2/3 cup dried cranberries

Directions:

1   Add all ingredients to machine pan except the cranberries.

2   Place pan into the oven chamber.

3   Select basic bread setting.

4   At the signal to add ingredients, add in the cranberries.

Nutrition:

225 Calories

7.8 g total fat

182 mg sodium

33 g carb.

1 fiber

6g protein

## 241. Sauerkraut Rye Bread

Preparation Time: 5 minutes

Cooking Time: 3 hours

Servings: 1 loaf

Difficulty: Beginners

Ingredients:

- 1 cup sauerkraut – rinsed and drained

- 3/4 cup warm water

- 1 ½ tablespoons molasses

- 1 ½ tablespoons butter

- 1 ½ tablespoons brown sugar

- 1 tsp caraway seed

- 1 ½ tsp salt

- 1 cup rye flour

- cups bread flour

- 1 ½ tsp active dry yeast

Directions:

1   Add all ingredients to machine pan.

2   Select basic bread setting.

Nutrition:

74 Calories

1.8 g total fat (0 g sat. fat)

4 mg Chol.

411 mg sodium

12 g carb

1 fiber

1.8 g protein

## 242.   Cheese Cauliflower Broccoli Bread

Preparation Time: 10 minutes

Cooking Time: 3 hours

Servings: 1 loaf

Difficulty: Beginners

Ingredients:

- 1/4 cup water
- tablespoons oil
- 1 egg white
- 1 tsp lemon juice

- 2/3 cup grated cheddar cheese

- Tablespoons green onion

- 1/2 cup broccoli, chopped

- 1/2 cup cauliflower, chopped

- 1/2 tsp lemon-pepper seasoning

- cup bread flour

- 1 tsp regular or quick-rising yeast

Directions:

1  Add all ingredients to machine pan.

2  Select basic bread setting.

Nutrition:

156 Calories

7.4 g total fat (2.2 g sat. fat)

8 mg Chol

, 56 mg sodium

17 g carb.

0 fiber

4,9 g protein

## 243.  Orange Cappuccino Bread

Preparation Time: 10 Minutes

Cooking Time: 3 Hours

Servings: 1 Loaf

Difficulty: Beginners

Ingredients:

- 1 cup water
- 1 tablespoon instant coffee granules
- tablespoons butter or margarine, softened
- 1 tsp grated orange peel
- cups Bread flour
- tablespoons dry milk
- 1/4 cup sugar
- 1 ¼ tsp of salt
- ¼ tsp of bread machine or quick active dry yeast

Directions :

1   Add all ingredients to machine pan.

2   Select basic bread setting.

Nutrition:

155 Calories

2 g total fat

5 mg Chol

270 mg sodium

31 g carb

1 fiber

4 g protein

# 244.  Anise Almond Bread

Preparation Time: 10 minutes

Cooking Time: 3 hours

Servings: 1 loaf

Difficulty: Beginners

Ingredients:

- 3/4 cup water
- 1 or 1/4 cup egg substitute
- 1/4 cup butter or margarine, softened
- 1/4 cup sugar
- 1/2 tsp salt
- cup bread flour
- 1 tsp anise seed
- tsp active dry yeast
- 1/2 cup almonds, chopped small

Directions:

1  Add all ingredients to machine pan except almonds.

2  Select basic bread setting.

3  After prompt, add almonds.

Nutrition:

78 Calories

4 g total fat (1 g sat. fat

, 4 mg Chol.

182 mg sodium

7 g carb.

0 fiber

4 g protein


## 245. Cottage Cheese Bread

Preparation Time: 10 Minutes

Cooking Time: 3 Hours

Servings: 1 Loaf

Difficulty: Beginners

Ingredients :

- 1/2 cup water
- 1 cup cottage cheese
- tablespoons margarine
- 1 egg
- 1 tablespoon white sugar
- 1/4 tsp baking soda
- 1 tsp salt
- cups bread flour
- ½ tsp active dry yeast

Directions:

1  Add all ingredients to machine pan. Use the order suggested by manufacturer.

2  Select basic bread setting.

3   Tip: If dough is too sticky, add up to ½ cup more flour.

Nutrition:

171 Calories

3.6 g total fat (1 g sat. fat)

18 mg Chol.

234 mg sodium

26 g carb.

1 fiber

7.3 g protein

## 246.   Vegetable Spoon Bread

Preparation Time: 10 Minutes

Cooking Time: 35 Minutes

Serving: 9

Difficulty: Beginners

Ingredients:

- 1 (10 ounce) package frozen chopped spinach, thawed and squeezed dry
- eggs, beaten
- 1 (8 ounce) can cream-style corn
- 1 cup low-fat sour cream
- 1/4 cup margarine, melted

1 (8.5 ounce) package corn muffin mix

Directions:

1   Preheat the oven at temperature 350 degrees F (175 degrees C). Grease a 9-inch square baking dish.

2   In a giant bowl, stir together the spinach, eggs, corn, sour cream and margarine until well blended. Stir in the dry cornbread mix. Dispense into the prepared pan, and spread evenly.

3   Bake for 35 minutes in the preheated oven, or until firm and slightly browned on the top.

Nutrition:

Calories: 226

Total Fat: 12.2 g

Cholesterol: 53 mg

Sodium: 605 mg

Total Carbohydrate: 24.8 g

Protein: 5.9 g


## 247.   Waikiki Cornbread

Preparation Time: 15 Minutes

Cooking Time: 30 Minutes

Serving: 15

Difficulty: Beginners

Ingredients:

- cups buttermilk baking mix

- 1 cup white sugar

- 1/2 teaspoons baking powder

- 1/4 cup yellow cornmeal

- eggs

- 1 1/4 cups milk

- 1 cup butter, melted

Directions :

1   Preheat oven at temperature  350 degrees F (175 degrees C). Lightly grease a 9x13 inch baking pan.

2   In a giant mixing bowl, combine baking mix, sugar, baking powder and cornmeal.

3   In a separate bowl, combine eggs, milk and melted butter; beat until creamy. Stir in flour mixture until well combined. Pour batter into prepared pan.

4   Bake at temperature 350 degrees F (175 degrees C) for 30 minutes, or until a toothpick inserted into the center of the bread comes out clean. Serve warm.

Nutrition:

Calories: 295

Total Fat: 17.4 g

Cholesterol: 72 mg

Sodium: 498 mg

Total Carbohydrate: 31.3 g

Protein: 4.1 g

## 248.   Unleavened Cornbread

Preparation Time: 10 Minutes

Cooking Time: 25 Minutes

Serving: 12

Difficulty: Beginners

Ingredients:

- 1 cup cornmeal

- 1 cup all-purpose flour

- 1/4 cup white sugar

- 1 teaspoon salt

- 1 egg

- 1/4 cup shortening, melted

- 1 cup milk

Directions:

1  Preheat the oven at temperature 425 degrees F (220 degrees C). Lubricate a 12 cup muffin pan or line with muffin papers.

2  Using a large bowl, stir together the cornmeal, flour, sugar and salt. Make a well in the mid and pour in the egg, shortening and milk. Stir until well blended. Spoon batter into the prepared muffin cups.

3  Bake for 20 to 25 minutes until a toothpick inserted into the middle of a muffin comes out clean.

Nutrition:

Calories: 150

Total Fat: 5.4 g

Cholesterol: 17 mg

Sodium: 209 mg

Total Carbohydrate: 22.2 g

Protein: 3.1 g

## 249.  Vegan Corn Bread

Preparation Time: 10 Minutes

Cooking Time: 20 Minutes

Serving: 9

Difficulty: Beginners

Ingredients:

- 1 cup all-purpose flour

- 1 cup cornmeal

- 1/4 cup turbinado sugar

- 1 tablespoon baking powder

- 1 teaspoon salt

- 1 cup sweetened, plain soy milk

- 1/3 cup vegetable oil

- 1/4 cup soft silken tofu

Directions:

1   Preheat an oven at temperature 400 degrees F (200 degrees C). Lubricate a 7 inch square baking pan. Whisk together the flour, cornmeal, sugar, baking powder, and salt in a mixing bowl; set aside.

2   Place the soy milk, oil, and tofu into a blender. Cover, and puree until smooth. Make a well in the mid of the cornmeal mixture. Pour the pureed tofu into the well, then stir in the cornmeal mixture until just moistened. Dispense the batter into the prepared baking pan.

3   Bake in the preheated oven until a toothpick inserted into the center comes out clean, 20 to 25 minutes. Cut into 9 pieces, and serve warm.

Nutrition:

Calories: 218

Total Fat: 9.1 g

Cholesterol: 0 mg

Sodium: 438 mg

Total Carbohydrate: 30.3 g

Protein: 3.8 g

## 250.   German Black Bread

Preparation Time: 3 hours 50 minutes

Cooking Time: 0

Difficulty: Beginners

Servings: 10

Ingredients:

- 1 cup water plus 2 tablespoons water

- tablespoons apple cider vinegar

- tablespoons molasses

- 1 tablespoon sugar

- 1 teaspoon salt

- 1 teaspoon instant coffee

- ¼ teaspoon fennel seeds

- 1 tablespoon caraway seeds

- ½ ounce unsweetened chocolate

- ½ cup bran cereal flakes

- ½ cup bread flour

- ½ cup rye flour

- cups whole almond flour

- 1 package active dry yeast

Directions:

1  Put all of the bread ingredients in your bread machine in the order listed above starting with the water, and finishing with the yeast. Put the bread machine to the whole wheat function.

2  Check on the dough after about 5 minutes and make sure that it's a soft ball. Put water 1 tablespoon at a time if it's too dry, and add flour 1 tablespoon at a time if it's too wet.

3  When bread is done allow it cool on a wire rack.

Nutrition:

Calories: 102

Carbs: 3.8 g

Fiber: 3.4 g

Fat: 1.4 g

Protein: 5.0 g.

## 251.  Herb Focaccia Bread

Preparation Time: 3.5 hours

Cooking Time: 0

Servings: 8

Difficulty: Beginners

Ingredients:

- Dough:
- 1 cup water
- tablespoons canola oil
- 1 teaspoon salt
- 1 teaspoon dried basil
- cups bread flour
- teaspoons bread machine yeast
- Topping:
- 1 tablespoon canola oil
- ½ cup fresh basil
- cloves garlic (to taste)
- tablespoons grated parmesan cheese
- 1 pinch salt

- 1 tablespoon cornmeal (optional)

Directions:

1. Put all of the bread ingredients in your bread machine, in the order listed above starting with the water, and finishing with the yeast. Make a well in mid of the flour and place the yeast in the well. Make sure the well doesn't touch any liquid. Put the bread machine to the dough function.

2. Check on the dough after about 5 minutes and make sure that it's a soft ball. Put water 1 tablespoon at a time if it's too dry, and add flour 1 tablespoon at a time if it's too wet.

3. When dough is ready set it on a lightly floured hard surface. Place a cover it and let it rest for 10 minutes.

4. While the dough is resting, chop up the garlic and basil, grease a 13x9 inch pan and evenly distribute cornmeal on top of it.

5. Once the dough has rested, press it into the greased pan. Drizzle oil on the dough and evenly distribute the salt parmesan, garlic, and basil.

Nutrition:

Calories: 108

Carbs: 37.4 g

Fiber: 1.6 g

Fat: 7.3 g

Protein: 7.7 g

## 252.  Jalapeno Loaf

Preparation time: 10 minutes

Cooking time: 22 minutes

Servings: 6

Difficulty: Beginners

Ingredients:

- 1 and ½ cups almond flour
- ½ cup flaxseed meal
- A pinch of salt
- teaspoons baking powder
- tablespoons butter, melted
- ½ cup sour cream
- eggs
- drops stevia
- jalapenos, chopped
- ½ cup cheddar, grated

Cooking spray

Directions:

1  Using a bowl, mix the flour with flaxseed meal, salt, baking powder, stevia, jalapenos and the cheese and stir.

2  Put the remaining ingredients and mix them until you obtain a dough.

3  Transfer it to a loaf pan greased with cooking spray and bake at 375 degrees f for 22 minutes.

4  Cool the bread down, slice and serve.

Nutrition:

calories 300

fat 20

fiber 3

carbs 4

protein 12

### 253. Cheesy Broccoli Bread

Preparation time: 10 minutes

Cooking time: 15 minutes

Servings: 2

Difficulty: Beginners

Ingredients:

- Cooking spray
- 1 egg
- 1 tablespoon coconut flour
- 1 tablespoon almond flour
- 1 tablespoon almond milk
- 1 tablespoon butter, melted
- ¼ teaspoon baking powder
- A pinch of salt
- 1 tablespoon broccoli, chopped
- 1 tablespoon mozzarella, grated

Directions:

1. By means of a bowl, mix the almond flour with the coconut flour, baking powder, salt, broccoli and the mozzarella and stir.

2. Put the remaining ingredients except the cooking spray and stir everything really well.

3   Grease a loaf pan with cooking spray, pour the bread batter, cook at 400 degrees f for 15 minutes, cool down and serve.

Nutrition:

calories 244

fat 20

fiber 4

carbs 6

protein 6

## 254. Dutch Oven Bread

Preparation time: 20 minutes

Cooking time: 30 minutes

Servings: 6

Difficulty: Beginners

Ingredients:

- 1 teaspoon baking powder
- 1 teaspoon baking soda
- cups almond flour
- 1 and ½ cups warm water
- A pinch of salt
- 1 teaspoon stevia

Directions:

1   Using a bowl, mix the water with the flour and stir well.

2   Add the rest of the ingredients, stir until you obtain a dough and leave aside for 20 minutes.

3   Transfer the dough to a dutch oven and bake the bread at 400 degrees f for 30 minutes.

4   Cool the bread down, slice and serve.

Nutrition:

calories 143

fat 9

fiber 3

carbs 4

protein 6

## 255.   Artichoke Bread

Preparation time: 10 minutes

Cooking time: 30 minutes

Servings: 10

Difficulty: Beginners

Ingredients:

- oz canned artichoke hearts
- 1 garlic clove, minced
- 1 cup parmesan, grated
- 1 cup almond flour
- ½ teaspoon baking powder
- 1 and ½ cups warm water

Directions:

1   Using a bowl, mix the flour with baking powder, and the water and stir well.

2   Add the rest of the ingredients, stir the dough well and transfer it to a lined round pan.

3   Bake at temperature 360 degrees f for 30 minutes, cool the bread down, slice and serve.

Nutrition:

calories 211

fat 12,

fiber 3

carbs 5

protein 6

## 256.   Keto Spinach Bread

Preparation time: 10 minutes

Cooking time: 30 minutes

Servings: 10

Difficulty: Beginners

Ingredients:

- ½ cup spinach, chopped
- 1 tablespoon olive oil
- 1 cup water
- cups almond flour
- A pinch of salt and black pepper
- 1 tablespoon stevia

- 1 teaspoon baking powder

- 1 teaspoon baking soda

- ½ cup cheddar, shredded

Directions:

1   Using a bowl, mix the flour, with salt, pepper, stevia, baking powder, baking soda and the cheddar and stir well.

2   Add the remaining ingredients, stir the batter really well and pour it into a lined loaf pan.

3   Cook at temperature 350 degrees f for 30 minutes, cool the bread down, slice and serve.

Nutrition:

calories 142

fat 7

fiber 3,

carbs 5

protein 6

## 257.   Cinnamon Asparagus Bread

Preparation time: 10 minutes

Cooking time: 45 minutes

Servings: 8

Difficulty: Beginners

Ingredients:

- 1 cup stevia

- ¾ cup coconut oil, melted

- 1 and ½ cups almond flour

- eggs, whisked

- A pinch of salt

- 1 teaspoon baking soda

- 1 teaspoon cinnamon powder

- cups asparagus, chopped

- Cooking spray

Directions:

1   Using a bowl, mix all the ingredients except the cooking spray and stir the batter really well.

2   Pour this batter into a loaf pan greased with cooking spray and bake at 350 degrees f for 45 minutes, cool the bread down, slice and serve.

Nutrition:

calories 165

fat 6

fiber 3

carbs 5

protein 6

## 258.   Kale and Cheese Bread

Preparation time: 10 minutes

Cooking time: 1 hour

Servings: 8

Difficulty: Beginners

Ingredients:

- cups kale, chopped
- 1 cup warm water
- 1 teaspoon baking powder
- 1 teaspoon baking soda
- tablespoons olive oil
- teaspoons stevia
- 1 cup parmesan, grated
- cups almond flour
- A pinch of salt
- 1 egg
- tablespoons basil, chopped

Directions:

1. Using a bowl, mix the flour, salt, parmesan, stevia, baking soda and baking powder and stir.

2. Put the rest of the ingredients gradually and stir the dough well.

3. Transfer it to a lined loaf pan, cook at 350 degrees f for 1 hour, cool down, slice and serve.

Nutrition:

calories 231

fat 7

fiber 2

carbs 5

protein 7

## 259.  Beet Bread

Preparation time: 1 hour and 10 minutes

Cooking time: 35 minutes

Servings: 6

Difficulty: Beginners

Ingredients:

- 1 cup warm water
- and ½ cups almond flour
- 1 and ½ cups beet puree
- tablespoons olive oil
- A pinch of salt
- 1 teaspoon stevia
- 1 teaspoon baking powder
- 1 teaspoon baking soda

Directions:

1   Using a bowl, combine the flour with the water and beet puree and stir well.

2   Add the rest of the ingredients, stir the dough well and pour it into a lined loaf pan.

3   Let the mix to rise in a warm place for 1 hour, and then bake the bread at temperature 375 degrees f for 35 minutes.

4   Cool the bread down, slice and serve.

Nutrition:

calories 200

fat 8

fiber 3

carbs 5

protein 6

## 260. Keto Celery Bread

Preparation time: 2 hours and 10 minutes

Cooking time: 35 minutes

Servings: 6

Difficulty: Beginners

Ingredients:

- ½ cup celery, chopped
- cups almond flour
- 1 teaspoon baking powder
- 1 teaspoon baking soda
- A pinch of salt
- tablespoons coconut oil, melted
- ½ cup celery puree

Directions:

1  Using a bowl, mix the flour with salt, baking powder and baking soda and stir.

2  Add the rest of the ingredients, stir the dough well, cover the bowl and keep in a warm place for 2 hours.

3   Move the dough to a lined loaf pan and cook at 400 degrees f for 35 minutes.

4   Cool the bread down, slice and serve.

Nutrition:

calories 162

fat 6

fiber 2

carbs 6

protein 4

## 261.   Easy Cucumber Bread

Preparation time: 10 minutes

Cooking time: 50 minutes

Servings: 6

Difficulty: Beginners

Ingredients:

- 1 cup erythritol
- 1 cup coconut oil, melted
- 1 cup almonds, chopped
- 1 teaspoon vanilla extract
- A pinch of salt
- A pinch of nutmeg, ground
- ½ teaspoon baking powder
- A pinch of cloves

- eggs
- 1 teaspoon baking soda
- 1 tablespoon cinnamon powder
- cups cucumber, peeled, deseeded and shredded
- cups coconut flour
- Cooking spray

Directions:

1. Using a bowl, mix the flour with cucumber, cinnamon, baking soda, cloves, baking powder, nutmeg, salt, vanilla extract and the almonds and stir well.

2. Put the rest of the ingredients except the coconut flour, stir well and transfer the dough to a loaf pan greased with cooking spray.

3. Bake at temperature of 325 degrees f for 50 minutes, cool the bread down, slice and serve.

Nutrition:

calories 243

fat 12

fiber 3

carbs 6

protein 7

## 262.  Red Bell Pepper Bread

Preparation time: 10 minutes

Cooking time: 30 minutes

Servings: 12

Difficulty: Beginners

Ingredients:

- 1 and ½ cups red bell peppers, chopped
- 1 teaspoon baking powder
- 1 teaspoon baking soda
- tablespoons warm water
- 1 and ¼ cups parmesan, grated
- A pinch of salt
- cups almond flour
- tablespoons ghee, melted
- 1/3 cup almond milk
- 1 egg

Directions:

1. Using a bowl, mix the flour with salt, parmesan, baking powder, baking soda and the bell peppers and stir well.
2. Put the rest of the ingredients and stir the bread batter well.
3. Transfer it to a lined loaf pan and bake at 350 degrees f for 30 minutes.
4. Cool the bread down, slice and serve.

Nutrition:

calories 100

fat 5

fiber 1

carbs 4

protein 4

## 263.  Tomato Bread

Preparation time: 1 hour and 10 minutes

Cooking time: 35 minutes

Servings: 12

Difficulty: Beginners

Ingredients:

- cups almond flour

- ½ teaspoon basil, dried

- ¼ teaspoon rosemary, dried

- 1 teaspoon oregano, dried

- ½ teaspoon garlic powder

- tablespoons olive oil

- cups tomato juice

- ½ cup tomato sauce

- 1 teaspoon baking powder

- 1 teaspoon baking soda

- tablespoons swerve

Directions:

1  Using a bowl, mix the flour with basil, rosemary, oregano and garlic and stir.

2  Put the rest of the ingredients and stir the batter well.

3  Pour into a lined loaf pan, cover and keep in a warm place for 1 hour.

4　Bake the bread at temperature 375 degrees f for 35 minutes, cool down, slice and serve.

Nutrition:

calories 102

fat 5

fiber 3

carbs 7

protein 4

# Chapter 19.  Other Bread Machine Recipes

### 264.  Fruit Bread

Preparation time: 3 hours

Cooking Time: 0

Servings: 8

Difficulty: Beginners

Ingredients:

- 1 egg

- 1 cup milk

- tablespoons rum

- ¼ cup butter

- ¼ cup brown sugar

- cups almond flour

- 1 tablespoon instant yeast

- 1 teaspoon salt

- Fruits:

- ¼ cups dried apricots, coarsely chopped

- ¼ cups prunes, coarsely chopped

- ¼ cups candied cherry, pitted

- ½ cups seedless raisins

- ¼ cup almonds, chopped

Directions:

1   Put all of the ingredients to your bread machine, carefully following the instructions of the manufacturer (except fruits).

2   Set the program of your bread machine to basic/sweet and set crust type to light or medium.

3   Press starts.

4   Once the machine beeps, add fruits.

5   Wait until the cycle completes.

6   Once the loaf is ready, take the bucket out and let the loaf cool for 5 minutes.

7   Gently shake the bucket to remove loaf.

8   Move it to a cooling rack, slice and serve.

9   Enjoy!

Nutrition:

carbohydrates 5 g

fats 10.9 g

protein 10.8 g

calories 441

## 265.   Marzipan Cherry Bread

Preparation time: 3 hours

Cooking Time: 0

Servings: 8

Difficulty: Beginners

Ingredients:

1 egg

- ¾ cup milk
- 1 tablespoon almond liqueur
- tablespoons orange juice
- ½ cup ground almonds
- ¼ cup butter
- 1/3 cup sugar
- cups almond flour
- 1 tablespoon instant yeast
- 1 teaspoon salt
- ½ cup marzipan
- ½ cup dried cherries, pitted

Directions:

1  Put all of the ingredients to your bread machine, carefully following the instructions of the manufacturer (except marzipan and cherry).

2  Set the program of your bread machine to basic/sweet and set crust type to light or medium.

3  Press starts.

4  Once the machine beeps, add marzipan and cherry.

5  Wait until the cycle completes.

6  Once the loaf is ready, take the bucket out and let the loaf cool for 5 minutes.

7  Gently shake the bucket to remove loaf.

8  Move it to a cooling rack, slice and serve.

Enjoy!

Nutrition:

carbohydrates 4.2 g

fats 16.4 g

protein 12.2 g

calories 511

## 266.   Ginger Prune Bread

Preparation time: 3 hours

Cooking Time: 0

Servings: 8

Difficulty: Beginners

Ingredients:

- eggs
- 1 cup milk
- ¼ cup butter
- ¼ cup sugar
- cups almond flour
- 1 tablespoon instant yeast
- 1 teaspoon salt
- 1 cup prunes, coarsely chopped
- 1 tablespoon fresh ginger, grated

Directions:

1    Put all of the ingredients to your bread machine, carefully following the instructions of the manufacturer (except ginger and prunes).

2    Set the program of your bread machine to basic/sweet and set crust type to light or medium.

3    Press starts.

4    Once the machine beeps, add ginger and prunes.

5    Wait until the cycle completes.

6    Once the loaf is ready, take the bucket out and let the loaf cool for 5 minutes.

7    Gently shake the bucket to remove loaf.

8    Move it to a cooling rack, slice and serve.

9    Enjoy!

Nutrition:

carbohydrates 4 g

fats 8.3 g

protein 10.1 g

calories 387

## 267.   Lemon Fruit Bread

Preparation time: 3 hours

Cooking Time: 0

Servings: 8

Difficulty: Beginners

Ingredients:

- 1 egg

- 1 cup milk

- ¼ cup butter

- 1/3 cup sugar

- cups almond flour

- 1 tablespoon instant yeast

- 1 teaspoon salt

- ½ cup candied lemons

- 1½ teaspoon lemon zest, grated

- ½ cup raisins

- ½ cup cashew nuts

Directions:

1. Put all of the ingredients to your bread machine, carefully following the instructions of the manufacturer (except fruits, zest, and nuts).

2. Set the program of your bread machine to basic/sweet and set crust type to light or medium.

3. Press starts.

4. Once the machine beeps, add fruits, zest, and nuts.

5. Wait until the cycle completes.

6. Once the loaf is ready, take the bucket out and let the loaf cool for 5 minutes.

7. Gently shake the bucket to remove loaf.

8. Move to a cooling rack, slice and serve.

Enjoy!

Nutrition:

carbohydrates 3.9 g

fats 10.6 g

protein 10 g

calories 438

Total fat 10.6

saturated fat 4.9 g

cholesterol 38 mg

## 268. Potato Rosemary Bread

Preparation time: 3 ½ hours

Cooking Time: 0

Servings: 8

Difficulty: Beginners

Ingredients:

- cups wheat flour

- 1 tablespoon sugar

- 1 tablespoon oil

- 1 ½ teaspoons salt

- 1 ½ cups water

- 1 teaspoon dry yeast

- 1 cup mashed potatoes, ground through a sieve

- Crushed rosemary

Directions:

1   Measure the required amount of ingredients. Install the mixing paddle in the baking container.

2   Fill with flour, salt, and sugar.

3   Add sunflower oil and water.

4   Close the lid, and put the yeast in the specially designated hole.

5   Set the mode of baking bread with a filling, according to the instructions of the bread maker.

6   When the dough knits and comes up the right number of times, a beep will sound, which means that you can add additional ingredients.

7   After the oven is finished, immediately remove the bread from the baking container.

Nutrition:

carbohydrates 5 g

fats 2.8 g

protein 7.4 g

calories 276

## 269.  Homemade Omega-3 Bread

Preparation time: 3 ½ hours

Cooking Time: 0

Servings: 8

Difficulty: Beginners

Ingredients:

- 3/5 cup milk

- ½ cup water

- eggs

- tablespoons rapeseed oil

- cups almond flour

- 1 cup flax flour

- teaspoons dry yeast

- teaspoons salt

- tablespoons cane sugar

- tablespoons flaxseeds

- 1 tablespoon sesame seeds

Directions:

1  Soak the flaxseeds in cool water for 30 minutes.

2  Combine all the liquid ingredients in the bread pan, then add sifted almond flour, flaxseed flour, yeast, sugar, and salt.

3  Set it to the basic program.

4  After the signal sounds, add sesame seeds and strained flaxseeds.

Nutrition:

carbohydrates 4.5 g

fats 9 g

protein 11.1 g

calories 289


## 270.  Ham & Cheese Rolls

Preparation time: 20 minutes

Cooking Time: 0

Servings: 6 rolls

Difficulty: Beginners

Ingredients:

- 0.5 cup cheddar cheese, shredded

- 1 cup deli ham, diced

- 0.75 cup mozzarella cheese, shredded

- large eggs

- 0.5 cup parmesan cheese, grated

- Standard sized flat sheet

Directions:

1   Heat the stove to the temperature of 375° Fahrenheit. Prepare a flat sheet with a layer of baking lining.

2   Blend the diced ham, eggs, mozzarella, and cheddar cheese in a glass dish until integrated well.

3   Heat for approximately 18 minutes in the stove until they turn slightly golden.

4   Enjoy immediately.

Nutrition:

protein: 17 grams

net carbs: 3 gram

fat: 13 grams

sugar: 1 gram,

calories: 198

## 271.   Low Carb Carrot Bread

Preparation time: 4 hours 5 minutes

Cooking Time: 0

Servings: 1 loaf

Difficulty: Beginners

Ingredients:

- teaspoons of cinnamon.

- 1/2 teaspoon of ginger.

- 1/4 teaspoon of nutmeg.

- tablespoons of granulated sweetener.

- 1/3 cup of unsweetened almond milk.

- 1/2 cup of melted butter.

- 1 teaspoon of vanilla extract.

- 1 teaspoon of maple extract.

- 1/2 teaspoon of apple cider vinegar.

- large eggs.

- 1 ounce of shredded carrots.

Directions:

1  Using a bread machine, add in the flour, baking powder, xanthan gum, baking soda, cinnamon, ginger, nutmeg, sweetener, almond milk, butter, vanilla extract, maple extract, vinegar, eggs, shredded carrots, and salt to taste in the order recommended by the machine manufacturer.

2  Set the bread machine to basic bread, select the crust color and loaf size if desired then bake the carrot bread according to the instructions on the machine.

3  Once baked, place the bread on a rack to cool for a few minutes, slice and serve.

Nutrition:

128 calories

fat 15g

carbohydrates 5g

protein 5g

## 272.  Raisin Bread Delis

Preparation time: 1 hour 30 minutes

Cooking time: 0

Servings 15 slices

Difficulty: Beginners

Ingredients:

- 1/2 cup of coconut flour.

- 1/2 cup of almond flour.

- tablespoons of psyllium husk powder.

- 1/4 cup of chopped raisins.

- tablespoons of swerve.

- 1 tablespoon of baking powder.

- 1/2 teaspoon of ground cinnamon.

- 1/4 teaspoon of salt to taste.

- cups of egg whites.

- tablespoons of melted butter.

- tablespoons of apple cider vinegar.

Directions:

1   Using a bread machine, add in the coconut flour, almond flour, psyllium husk powder, chopped raisins, sweetener, baking powder, cinnamon, egg whites, butter, vinegar, and salt to taste in the order recommended by the machine manufacturer then set the machine to basic bread setting.

2   Pick the crust color and loaf size if desired then bake the carrot bread according to the instructions on the machine.

3   Once baked, place the bread on a rack to cool for a few minutes, slice and serve.

Nutrition:

calories 132

fat 6.58g

carbohydrates 12.36g

fiber 6.02g

protein 6.28g.

## 273.   Amazing Buttery Dinner Buns

Preparation time:  3 hours 30 minutes

Cooking Time: 0

Servings: 15-20 Buns

Difficulty: Beginners

Ingredients:

- 1 cup water
- tablespoons butter
- 1 whole egg
- and ¼ cups bread flour
- ¼ cup sugar
- 1 teaspoon salt
- teaspoon active dry yeast

Directions:

1. Put all of the ingredients to your Bread Machine (except melted butter).

2. Set the program to "Dough" cycle and let the cycle run.

3. Remove the dough (using lightly floured hands) and carefully place it on a floured surface.

4. Cover with a light film/cling paper and let the dough rise for 10 minutes.

5. Take a large cookie sheet and grease with butter.

6. Cut the risen dough into 15-20 pieces and shape them into balls.

7. Place the balls onto the sheet (2 inches apart) and cover.

8. Place in a warm place and let them rise for 30-40 minutes until the dough doubles.

9. Preheat your oven at 375 degrees F, transfer the cookie sheet to your oven and bake for 12-15 minutes.

10. Brush the top with a bit of butter, enjoy!

Nutrition:

Calories: 135

Total Fat: 2g

Saturated Fat: 0g

Protein: 4g

Carbs: 26g

Fiber: 1g

Sugar: 10g

## 274. Delicious Multigrain Buns

Preparation time: 3 hours 30 minutes

Cooking Time: 0

Servings: 15-20 Buns

Difficulty: Beginners

Ingredients:

- Melted Butter for grease
- ½ tablespoons honey
- ½ teaspoon salt
- ½ cup multigrain flour
- 1 and ½ cups white bread flour
- 1 teaspoon active dry yeast

Directions:

1  Put all of the ingredients to your Bread Machine (except melted butter).

2  Set the program to "Dough" cycle and let the cycle run.

3  Remove the dough (using lightly floured hands) and carefully place it on a floured surface.

4  Cover with a light film/cling paper and let the dough rise for 10 minutes.

5  Take a large cookie sheet and grease with butter.

6  Cut the risen dough into 15-20 pieces and shape them into balls.

7  Place the balls onto the sheet (2 inches apart) and cover.

8  Place in a warm place and let them rise for 30-40 minutes until the dough doubles.

9  Brush the top with a bit of butter, enjoy!

Nutrition:

Calories: 145

Total Fat: 2g

Saturated Fat: 1g

Protein: 4g

Carbs: 27

Fiber: 1g

Sugar: 10g

## 275.  Lemon and Poppy Buns

Preparation time:  3 hours 30 minutes

Cooking Time: 0

Servings: 10-20 Buns

Difficulty: Beginners

Ingredients:

- Melted Butter for grease

- 1 and 1/3 cups hot water

- tablespoons powdered milk

- tablespoons Crisco shortening

- 1 and ½ teaspoon salt

- 1 tablespoon lemon juice

- and ¼ cups bread flour

- ½ teaspoon nutmeg

- teaspoons grated lemon rind

- tablespoons poppy seeds

- 1 and ¼ teaspoons yeast

- teaspoons wheat gluten

Directions:

1  Put all of the ingredients to your Bread Machine (except melted butter).

2  Set the program to "Dough" cycle and let the cycle run.

3  Remove the dough (using lightly floured hands) and carefully place it on a floured surface.

4  Cover with a light film/cling paper and let the dough rise for 10 minutes.

5  Take a large cookie sheet and grease with butter.

6  Cut the risen dough into 15-20 pieces and shape them into balls.

7  Place the balls onto the sheet (2 inches apart) and cover.

8  Place in a warm place and let them rise for 30-40 minutes until the dough doubles.

9  Preheat your oven at 375 degrees F, transfer the cookie sheet to your oven and bake for 12-15 minutes.

10 Brush the top with a bit of butter, enjoy!

Nutrition:

Calories: 231

Total Fat: 11g

Saturated Fat: 1g

Protein: 4g

Carbs: 31g

Fiber: 1g

Sugar: 12g

## 276.  Sweet Easter Bread

Preparation time: 5 minutes

Cooking time: 35 minutes

Servings: 20 slices

Difficulty: Beginners

Ingredients:

- teaspoons baking powder
- 1 cup water
- 1/2 cups almond flour
- 1/4 cup almond milk/ heavy cream
- cups whey isolate
- 1/2 cup sugar substitute
- 1/2 teaspoon salt
- 1/2 cup butter, melted
- teaspoons xanthan gum

Directions:

1   Add all ingredients to the Bread Machine.

2   Select Dough setting and press Start. Mix the ingredients for about 4-5 minutes. After that press Stop button.

3   Smooth out the top of the loaf. Choose Bake mode and press Start. Let it bake for about 30 minutes.

4   Remove bread from the bread machine and let it rest for 10 minutes. Enjoy!

Nutrition:

150 calories

11.6 g fat

3.4 g total carb

9.6 g protein

## 277. Zucchini Apple Fritter Bread

Preparation time: 5 minutes

Cooking time: 1 hour 10 minutes

Servings: 12 slices

Difficulty: Intermediate

Ingredients:

- teaspoons apple extract
- 1 medium zucchini peeled, seeded and chopped
- 1/4 cup Sorkin Gold
- 1/2 cup unsweetened almond milk
- 1 teaspoon cinnamon
- 1/2 teaspoon xanthan gum (optional)
- 1/2 cup low carb sugar substitute
- teaspoons baking powder
- 1/2 cup butter, softened
- 1/2 cup coconut flour
- eggs
- 1 cup almond flour
- Glaze:

- 2-3 tablespoons heavy cream

- 1/4 cup Sukrin Melis

Directions:

1   Add all ingredients to the Bread Machine.

2   Select Dough setting and press Start. Mix the ingredients for about 4-5 minutes. After that press Stop button.

3   Smooth out the top of the loaf. Choose Bake mode and press Start. Let it bake for about 50 minutes.

4   For glaze, mix together 2-3 tablespoons heavy cream and 1/4 cup

5   Remove bread from the bread machine, let it rest a little and drizzle glaze over zucchini apple fritter bread.

Nutrition:

171 calories

15 g fat

6 g total carbs

4 g protein

## 278.   Peanut Flour Bread

Preparation time: 5 minutes

Cooking time: 1 hour

Servings: 12

Difficulty: Intermediate

Ingredients:

- eggs

- 1 teaspoon baking powder

- 1/2 cup butter

- tsp guar gum/xanthan gum (optional)

- oz cream cheese

- 1 1/3 cups peanut flour

- 3/4 cup low carb sugar substitute

- 1 teaspoon vanilla extract

Directions:

1. Add all ingredients to the Bread Machine.

2. Select Dough setting and press Start. Mix the ingredients for about 4-5 minutes. After that press Stop button.

3. Smooth out the top of the loaf. Choose Bake mode and press Start. Let it bake for about 55 minutes.

4. Remove bread from the bread machine and let it rest for 10 minutes. Enjoy!

Nutrition:

152 calories

13 g fat

3 g total carbs

7 g protein

### 279.  Summer Squash Bread

Preparation time: 5 minutes

Cooking time: 45 minutes

Servings: 8

Difficulty: Intermediate

Ingredients:

- 1 teaspoon sugar-free vanilla extract

- 1 cup summer squash, shredded

- eggs, beaten

- 1/4 teaspoon ground nutmeg

- 1/2 cup Swerve or Sukrin

- 1 1/2 teaspoons ground cinnamon

- 1/4 cup butter, melted

- 1 1/2 teaspoons baking powder

- tablespoons vegetable oil

- 1 1/2 cups Carbquik

Directions:

1  Add all ingredients to the Bread Machine.

2  Select Dough setting and press Start. Mix the ingredients for about 4-5 minutes. After that press Stop button.

3  Smooth out the top of the loaf. Choose Bake mode and press Start. Let it bake for about 50 minutes.

4  Remove bread from the bread machine and let it rest for 10 minutes. Enjoy!

Nutrition:

154 calories

14 g fat

10 g total carbs

5 g protein

## 280.   Fathead Dough Bagels

Preparation time: 5 minutes

Cooking time: 12 minutes

Servings: 6 bagels

Difficulty: Intermediate

Ingredients:

- 1/2 cup mozzarella cheese, shredded

- sesame seeds (optional)

- 1 1/2 cup blanched almond flour

- large beaten eggs

- 1 tablespoon gluten-free baking powder

- oz. cream cheese, cubed

Directions:

1   Line baking sheet with parchment paper.

2   Add all ingredients to the Bread Machine.

3   Select Dough setting. When the time is over, transfer the dough to the floured surface. Shape it into a ball and cut into about 6 even pieces.

4   Form a long log with every part and join both ends, forming a bagel shape, then place on a baking sheet. Form all bagels in this way.

5   Sprinkle bagels with sesame seeds and press them gently into dough, if needed.

6   Bake in a preheated oven at 400 F until golden and firm, for about 10-14 minutes.

Nutrition:

360 calorie

28 g fat

8 g total carbs

21 g protein

## 281. Coconut Rolls

Preparation time: 5 minutes

Cooking time: 25 minutes

Servings: 10 rolls

Difficulty: Intermediate

Ingredients:

- 1/4 teaspoon pink Himalayan salt
- tablespoons butter
- 1/2 cup coconut flour
- large eggs
- tablespoons psyllium husk powder
- 3/4 cup water
- 1/2 teaspoon baking powder

Directions:

1   Line baking sheet with parchment paper.

2   Add all ingredients to the Bread Machine.

3   Select Dough setting. When the time is over, transfer the dough to the floured surface. Shape it into a ball and cut into about 10 even pieces.

4   Bake at temperature of 350 F for about 30-35 minutes.

Nutrition:

102 calorie

7 g fat

5.8 g total carbs

3 g protein

## 282.   Cauliflower Bread

Preparation time: 5 minutes

Cooking time: 50 minutes

Servings: 10 slices

Difficulty: Intermediate

Ingredients:

- tablespoons canola oil

- 1 teaspoon salt

- cups cauliflower finely riced, microwaved for 3-4 minutes

- 1 tablespoon baking powder

- large eggs, separated

- 1 ¼ cups of superfine almond flour

Directions:

1   Add all ingredients to the Bread Machine.

2   Select Dough setting and press Start. Mix the ingredients for about 4-5 minutes. After that press Stop button.

3   Smooth out the top of the loaf. Choose Bake mode and press Start. Let it bake for about 45 minutes.

4   Remove bread from the bread machine and let it rest for 10 minutes. Enjoy!

Nutrition:

204 calories

17 g fat

6 g total carbs

7 g protein

## 283.   Avocado Bread

Preparation time: 5 minutes

Cooking time: 45 minutes

Servings: 10 slices

Difficulty: Intermediate

Ingredients:

- 1 tablespoon vanilla extract

- tablespoons cocoa powder unsweetened (optional)

- 1 1/2 cups avocado mashed, ripe

- 1/2 teaspoon salt

- tablespoons monk fruit/erythritol blend sweetener

- 3/4 teaspoon baking soda

- eggs large

- tablespoons coconut flour

Directions:

1 Add all ingredients to the Bread Machine.

2 Select Dough setting and press Start. Mix the ingredients for about 4-5 minutes. After that press Stop button.

3 Smooth out the top of the loaf. Choose Bake mode and press Start. Let it bake for about 40 minutes.

4 Remove bread from the bread machine and let it rest for 10 minutes. Enjoy!

Nutrition:

100 calories

7.3 g fat

5.7 g total carbs

3.2 g protein

# 284.  Poppy-Seed Bread

Preparation time: 5 minutes

Cooking time: 30 minutes

Servings: 8

Difficulty: Intermediate

Ingredients:

- tablespoons sunflower seeds

- 1 tablespoon poppy seeds

- oz. cottage cheese

- 1 teaspoon sea salt

- eggs

- 1 teaspoon ground psyllium husk powder

- 1 tablespoon olive oil

- 1 teaspoon baking powder

- tablespoons chia seeds or flaxseed

Directions:

1. Add all ingredients to the Bread Machine.

2. Select Dough setting and press Start. Mix the ingredients for about 4-5 minutes. After that press Stop button.

3. Smooth out the top of the loaf. Choose Bake mode and press Start. Let it bake for about 25 minutes.

4. Remove bread from the bread machine and let it rest for 10 minutes. Enjoy!

Nutrition:

127 calories

9 g fat

2 g total carbs

7 g protein

## 285. Greek Olive Bread

Preparation Time: 15 minutes

Cooking Time: 0

Servings: 20

Difficulty: Intermediate

Ingredients:

- eggs
- tbsps. ground flaxseed
- tsp psyllium powder

- tbsps. apple cider vinegar

- 1 tsp baking soda

- 1 tsp salt

- ½ cup sour cream

- ½ cup olive oil

- oz black olives, chopped

- 1 tsp ground rosemary

- 1 ½ cups almond flour

- 1 tsp dried basil

Directions:

1. Beat eggs in a mixing bowl for about 5 minutes. Add olive oil slowly while you continue to beat the eggs. Add in sour cream and apple cider vinegar and continue to beat for another 5 minutes.

2. Combine all of the remaining ingredients together in a separate smaller bowl.

3. Place all wet ingredients into bread machine pan.

4. Put the remaining ingredients to the bread pan.

5. Set bread machine to the French setting.

6. When the bread is done, remove bread machine pan from the bread machine.

7. Cool to some extent before moving to a cooling rack.

8. The bread can be kept for up to 7 days on the counter.

Nutrition:

Calories: 150

Carbohydrates: 3g

Protein: 3g

Fat: 14g

## 286. Veggie Loaf

Preparation Time: 20 minutes

Cooking Time: 0

Servings: 20

Difficulty: Intermediate

Ingredients:

- 1/3 cup coconut flour
- tablespoons chia Seed
- tbsps. psyllium husk powder
- ¼ cup sunflower seeds
- ¼ cup pumpkin seeds
- tbsp flax seed
- 1 cup almond flour
- 1 cup zucchini, grated
- eggs
- ¼ cup coconut oil, melted
- 1 tbsp paprika
- tsp cumin
- tsp baking powder
- tsp salt

Directions:

1.  Grate carrots and zucchini, use a cheesecloth to drain excess water, set aside.

2.  Mix eggs and coconut oil into bread machine pan.

3.  Add the remaining ingredients to bread pan.

4.  Set bread machine to quick bread setting.

5.  When the bread is done, remove bread machine pan from the bread machine.

6.  Cool to some extent before transferring to a cooling rack.

7.  You can store your veggie loaf bread for up to 5 days in the refrigerator, or you can also be sliced and stored in the freezer for up to 3 months.

Nutrition:

Calories: 150

Carbohydrates: 3g

Protein: 3g

Fat: 14g

## 287.  Cajun Veggie Loaf

Preparation Time: 15 minutes

Cooking Time: 0

Servings: 12

Difficulty: Intermediate

Ingredients:

- ½ cup water

- ¼ cup onion, chopped

- ½ cup green bell pepper, chopped

- tsp garlic, chopped finely

- tsp ghee

- cups almond flour

- 1 tbsp inulin

- 1 tsp Cajun seasoning

- 1 tsp active dry yeast

Directions:

1  Add water and ghee to bread machine pan.

2  Add in the remaining ingredients.

3  Set bread machine to basic setting.

4  When done, remove from bread machine and allow to cool before slicing.

5  Cool to some extent before transferring to a cooling rack.

6  You can store your bread for up to 5 days in the refrigerator.

Nutrition:

Calories: 101

Carbohydrates: 6g

Protein: 4g

Fat: 8g

## 288.  Parmesan Italian Bread

Preparation Time: 16 minutes

Cooking Time: 0

Servings: 10

Difficulty: Intermediate

Ingredients:

- 1 1/3 cup warm water
- tbsps. olive oil
- cloves of garlic, crushed
- 1 tbsp. basil
- 1 tbsp. oregano
- 1 tbsp. parsley
- cups almond flour
- 1 tbsp. inulin
- ½ cup parmesan cheese, grated
- 1 tsp active dry yeast

Directions:

- Dispense all wet ingredients into bread machine pan.
- Add all dry ingredients to pan.
- Set bread machine to French bread.
- When the bread is done, remove bread machine pan from the bread machine.
- Cool to some extent before transferring to a cooling rack.
- You can store your bread for up to 7 days.

Nutrition:

Calories: 150

Carbohydrates: 14g

Protein: 5g

Fat: 5g

## 289. Bacon Jalapeño Cheesy Bread

Preparation Time: 22 minutes

Cooking Time: 0

Servings: 12

Difficulty: Intermediate

Ingredients:

- 1 cup golden flaxseed, ground

- ¾ cup coconut flour

- tsp baking powder

- ¼ tsp black pepper

- 1 tbsp. erythritol

- 1/3 cup pickled jalapeno

- oz. cream cheese, full fat

- eggs

- cups sharp cheddar cheese, shredded + ¼ cup extra for the topping

- tbsps. parmesan cheese, grated

- 1 ¼ cup almond milk

- Bacon Slices (cooked and crumbled)

- ¼ cup rendered bacon grease (from frying the bacon)

Directions:

1 Cook the bacon in a larger frying pan, set aside to cool on paper towels. Save ¼ cup of bacon fat for the recipe, allow to cool slightly before using.

2 Add wet ingredients to bread machine pan, including the cooled bacon grease.

3 Add in the remaining ingredients.

4 Set the bread machine to the quick bread setting.

5 When the bread is done, remove bread machine pan from the bread machine.

6 Cool to some extent before transferring to a cooling rack.

7 Once on a cooling rack, top with the remaining cheddar cheese.

8 You can store your bread for up to 7 days.

Nutrition:

Calories: 235

Carbohydrates: 5g

Protein: 11g

Fat: 17g

## 290. Raspberry Bread

Preparation Time: 20 minutes

Cooking Time: 0

Difficulty: Intermediate

Servings: 10

Ingredients:

- cups almond flour

- ½ cup coconut flour

- ½ cup ghee

- ½ cup coconut oil, melted

- ½ cup erythritol

- eggs

1 tsp lemon juice

- ½ cup raspberries

- tsp baking powder

Directions:

1   Lightly beat eggs before pouring into bread machine pan.

2   Add in melted coconut oil, ghee, and lemon juice to pan.

3   Add the remaining ingredients.

4   Set bread machine to quick bread.

5   When the bread is done, remove bread machine pan from the bread machine.

6   Cool to some extent before transferring to a cooling rack.

7   You can store your bread for up to 5 days.

Nutrition:

Calories: 300

Carbohydrates: 14g

Protein: 5g

Fat: 30g

## 291.   Whole-Wheat Sourdough Bread

Preparation Time: 10 minutes

Cooking Time: 0

Servings: 8

Difficulty: Intermediate

Ingredients:

- ⅔ cups hot water

- ⅔ cup No-Yeast Whole-Wheat Sourdough Starter, fed, active, and at room temperature

- teaspoons butter, melted

- teaspoons sugar

- 1 teaspoon salt

- 1¼ teaspoons instant yeast

- cups whole- almond flour

Directions:

1  Put all ingredients in the bread machine.

2  Set the machine to Whole-Wheat/Whole-Grain bread, select light or medium crust, and press Start.

3  When ready, remove the bread and allow about 5 minutes to cool the loaf.

4  Put it on a rack to cool it completely

Nutrition:

Calories: 155

Fat: 2g

Carbohydrates: 2.9g

Fiber: 1g

Protein: 4g


## 292.  Blueberry Muffin Bread

Preparation Time: 15 minutes

Cooking Time: 0

Servings: 12

Difficulty: Intermediate

Ingredients:

- ½ cup almond butter

- 1/3 cup coconut oil

- ½ cup almond flour

- ½ cup erythritol

- ½ tsp salt

- tsp baking powder

- ½ cup almond milk, unsweetened

- eggs

- ½ cup blueberries

Directions:

1  Using a small microwaveable bowl, combine your almond butter and coconut oil. Heat for about 10 seconds to melt (it may need an extra 5 or more seconds to melt depending on your microwave).

2  Add the eggs into the bowl with the melted butter and oil and beat slightly.

3  Add the egg mixture into your bread machine pan.

4  Add the milk.

5  Use a separate small mixing bowl to combine all of your dry ingredients.

6  Pour dry ingredients on top of the wet mixture in your bread machine pan.

7  Set the bread machine to its basic bread setting.

8  Check the dough halfway through its kneading process to ensure it is smooth and tacky. If needed add a tablespoon more of flour if too wet, or a tablespoon of water if too dry.

9  Let the dough continue to knead and bake in the bread machine.

10  When the bread is done, remove bread machine pan from the bread machine.

11  Cool to some extent before transferring to a cooling rack.

12  You can store your bread for up to 4 days.

Nutrition:

Calories: 156

Carbohydrates: 4g

Protein: 5g

Fat: 13g

## 293.  Lemon Blueberry Bread

Preparation Time: 10 minutes

Cooking Time: 0

Servings: 10

Difficulty: Intermediate

Ingredients:

- cups almond flour

- ½ cup coconut flour

- ½ cup ghee

- ½ cup coconut oil, melted

- ½ cup erythritol

- eggs

- tbsps. lemon zest, about half a lemon

- 1 tsp lemon juice

- ½ cup blueberries

- tsp baking powder

Directions:

1   Lightly beat eggs before pouring into your bread machine pan.

2   Add in melted coconut oil, ghee, and lemon juice to pan.

3   Add the remaining dry ingredients including blueberries and lemon zest to the bread machine pan.

4   Set bread machine to quick bread setting.

5   When the bread is done, remove bread machine pan from the bread machine.

6   Cool to some extent before transferring to a cooling rack.

7   You can store your bread for up to 5 days.

Nutrition:

Calories: 300

Carbohydrates: 14g

Protein: 5g

Fat: 30g

## 294.   Cheese Blend Bread

Preparation Time: 25 minutes

Cooking Time: 0

Servings: 12

Difficulty: intermediate

Ingredients:

- oz. cream cheese

- ¼ cup ghee

- 2/3 cup almond flour

- ¼ cup coconut flour

- tbsps. whey protein, unflavored

- tsp baking powder

- ½ tsp Himalayan salt

- ½ cup parmesan cheese, shredded

- tbsps. water

- eggs

- ½ cup mozzarella cheese, shredded

Directions:

1  Place wet ingredients into bread machine pan.

2  Add dry ingredients.

3  Set the bread machine to the gluten free setting.

4  When the bread is done, remove bread machine pan from the bread machine.

5  Cool to some extent before transferring to a cooling rack.

6  You can store your bread for up to 5 days.

Nutrition:

Calories: 132

Carbohydrates: 4g

Protein: 6g

Fat: 8 g


## 295.  Strawberries and Cream Bread

Preparation Time: 18 minutes

Cooking Time: 0

Servings: 10

Difficulty: expert

Ingredients:

- ¾ cup whole milk
- ½ cup cream cheese
- ½ cup strawberries, sliced
- 1 tbsp. coconut oil, melted
- 1 tsp salt
- tbsps. inulin
- 1 tbsp. chia seeds
- cups almond Flour
- tsp instant yeast

Directions:

1. Dispense all wet ingredients into bread machine pan.
2. Add dry ingredients to pan.
3. Set bread machine to the sweet bread setting.
4. Check the dough while kneading to ensure more water does not need to be added. Otherwise just allow the bread machine to run its course.
5. When the bread is done, remove bread machine pan from the bread machine.
6. Cool to some extent before moving to a cooling rack.
7. You can store your bread for up to 5 days.

Nutrition:

Calories: 120

Carbohydrates: 5g

Protein: 4g

Fat: 10g

## 296.  3 Ingredient Breadsticks

Preparation Time: 35-40 minutes

Cooking Time: 0

Servings: 5

Difficulty: Intermediate

Ingredients:

- Dough:
- 1.5 cups of mozzarella cheese (shredded)
- eggs
- 1/8 tbsp. Italian seasoning
- Topping:
- Half cup of mozzarella cheese (shredded)
- tbsp. parmesan cheese (shredded, optional)
- 1/3 tbsp. parsley (finely chopped, optional)

Directions:

1   Make the oven ready for baking by heating it to a temperature of 350 degrees Fahrenheit. Get a sheet of parchment paper and line one square, nine-by-nine inch baking pan.

2   Put the cheese, seasoning and eggs in a food processor and blend until all the ingredients are mixed properly.

3   Scoop out the batter into the lined baking pan. Spread out the mixture so that it forms an even layer. Put it in the oven. Bake for 20 minutes until the crust becomes fairly firm and the dough is not wet at any place. Take it out of the oven and allow it to cool.

4   Heat the oven to a temperature of 425 degrees Fahrenheit.

5   Remove the crust from the parchment paper. Put it in on a cooling rack (oven safe rack). This will help to make the bottom part to become crisp.

6   Sprinkle the cheese meant for the topping. You can use either mozzarella or Parmesan cheese for this purpose.

7   Put the cooling rack in the oven. Cook for five minutes until the cheese melts.

8   Before you cut and serve the breadsticks you can garnish with parsley, if you like.

Nutrition:

2 Breadsticks:

Total calories: 142

Total fat: 9.2 grams

Fat (saturated): 4.9 grams

Cholesterol: 98.2 milligrams

Sodium: 297.1 milligrams

Carbohydrates: 3.1 grams

Fiber: 0.1 gram

Sugar: 0.9 grams

Protein: 11.4 grams

## 297.   Bread with Walnuts and Garlic

Preparation Time: 4 hours

Cooking Time: 0

Servings: 10

Difficulty: expert

Ingredients:

- cups almond flour
- teaspoons dry yeast
- 1 cup walnuts
- garlic cloves, chopped
- tablespoons Olive oil
- 1 cup garlic butter, melted
- cups water
- teaspoons sugar
- egg yolks
- Sea salt to taste

Directions:

1   Preheat the oven to 290°-320°Fahrenheit and roast the walnuts in the oven for 10-15 minutes until lightly browned and crispy. Set aside to cool completely. Grind the walnuts using a food processor.

2   Melt the unsalted butter by making it softer, by taking it out of the fridge and leaving for around 30 minutes or melt the butter using a frying pan. Meanwhile chop the garlic cloves.

3   Lubricate the surface of the dough with the water or the egg yolk.

4   Now close the lid and turn the bread machine on the basic/white bread program.

5   After the breakfast wheat bread with garlic is ready, take it out and leave for 1 hour covered with the towel and then you can consume the bread, although we recommend eating your bread after 24 hours.

Nutrition:

Calories: 100

Fat: 4g

Carbohydrates 4.6

Sugar 0g

Proteins: 2

## 298.   American Cheese Beer Bread

Preparation time: 5 minutes

Cooking time: 15 minutes

Servings: 10

Difficulty: Intermediate

Ingredients:

- ½ cups of fine almond flour
- tsp. Of unsalted melted butter
- salt, one teaspoon
- an egg
- swerve sweetener, two teaspoons
- keto low-carb beer, one cup
- ¾ tsp. Of baking powder
- ½ cup of cheddar cheese, shredded
- ½ tsp. Of active dry yeast

Directions:

1    Prepare a mixing container, where you will combine the almond flour, swerve sweetener, salt, shredded cheddar cheese, and baking powder.

2    Prepare another mixing container, where you will combine the unsalted melted butter, egg, and low- carb keto beer.

3    When the bread is ready, using oven mitts, remove the bread pan from the machine.

Nutrition:

Calories: 94

Fat: 6g

Carb: 4g

Protein: 1g

## 299.   Bread with Beef and Peanuts

Preparation time: 3 hours

Cooking Time: 0

Servings: 8

Difficulty: Intermediate

Ingredients:

- oz beef meat
- oz herbs de provence
- big onions
- cloves chopped garlic
- 1 cup of milk
- 20 oz almond flour

- oz rye flour

- teaspoons dry yeast

- 1 egg

- tablespoons sunflower oil

- 1 tablespoon sugar

- Sea salt

- Ground black pepper

- Red pepper

Directions:

1  Sprinkle the beef meat with the herbs de provence, salt, black, and red pepper and marinate in bear for overnight.

2  Cube the beef and fry in a skillet or a wok on medium heat until soft (for around 20 minutes).

3  Combine the beef pieces and the dough and mix in the bread machine.

4  Cover the lid and turn the bread machine on the basic program.

5  Bake the bread until the medium crust and after the bread is ready take it out and leave for 1 hour covered with the towel and only then you can slice the bread.

Nutrition:

carbohydrates 4 g

fats 42 g

protein 27 g

calories 369

## 300. Basic Sweet Yeast Bread

Preparation time: 3 hours

Cooking Time: 0

Servings: 8

Difficulty: Intermediate

Ingredients:

- 1 egg
- ¼ cup butter
- 1/3 cup sugar
- 1 cup milk
- ½ teaspoon salt
- cups almond flour
- 1 tablespoon active dry yeast
- After beeping:
- Fruits/ground nuts

Directions:

1 Put all of the ingredients to your bread machine, carefully following the instructions of the manufacturer (except fruits/ground nuts).

2 Set the program of your bread machine to basic/sweet and set crust type to light or medium.

3 Press starts.

4 Once the machine beeps, add fruits/ground nuts.

5 Wait until the cycle completes.

6 Once the loaf is ready, take the bucket out and let the loaf cool for 5 minutes.

7   Gently shake the bucket to remove loaf.

8   Move it to a cooling rack, slice and serve.

9   Enjoy!

Nutrition:

carbohydrates 2.7 g

fats 7.6 g

protein 8.8 g

calories 338

## 301.   Citrus Bread

Preparation time: 3 hours

Cooking Time: 0

Servings: 8

Difficulty: Intermediate

Ingredients:

- 1 egg
- tablespoons butter
- 1/3 cup sugar
- 1 tablespoon vanilla sugar
- ½ cup orange juice
- 2/3 cup milk
- 1 teaspoon salt
- cup almond flour

- 1 tablespoon instant yeast

- ¼ cup candied oranges

- ¼ cup candied lemon

- teaspoons lemon zest

- ¼ cup almond, chopped

Directions:

1   Put all of the ingredients to your bread machine, carefully following the instructions of the manufacturer (except candied fruits, zest, and almond).

2   Set the program of your bread machine to basic/sweet and set crust type to light or medium.

3   Press starts.

4   Once the machine beeps, add candied fruits, lemon zest, and chopped almonds.

5   Wait until the cycle completes.

6   Once the loaf is ready, take the bucket out and let the loaf cool for 5 minutes.

7   Gently shake the bucket to remove loaf.

8   Move it to a cooling rack, slice and serve.

9   Enjoy!

Nutrition:

carbohydrates 4 g

fats 9.1 g

protein 9.8 g

calories 404

# Conclusion

Depending on what kind of home baker you are, bread is either a must-know rite of passage, or an intimidating goal you haven't quite worked up the courage to try. This is because bread is a labor-intensive food where slight mistakes can have a big impact on the final result. Most of us rely on store-bought bread, but once you've tasted homemade bread, it's tempting to make your own as often as possible. A bread machine makes the process easier.

Making a loaf of bread feels like a major accomplishment. Why? There are a lot of steps. Mixing, kneading, proofing, resting, shaping, and finally baking.

You know how to make bread by hand, so how does the bread-making machine do it? A bread machine is basically a small, electric oven. It fits one large bread tin with a special axle connected to the electric motor. A metal paddle connects to the axle, and this is what kneads the dough. If you were making the bread in a mixer, you would probably use a dough hook, and in some instructions, you'll see the bread machine's kneading part referred as a hook or "blades."

The first thing you do is take out the tin and add the bread dough you made in Step 1. Bread machines can make any kind of bread, whether it's made from normal white flour, whole wheat, etc. Pop this tin unto the axle and program by selecting the type of bread, which includes options like basic, whole-wheat, multigrain, and so on. There are even cycles specifically for sweet breads; breads with nuts, seeds, and raisins; gluten-free; and bagels. Many models also let you cook jam.

You'll probably see a "dough" mode option, too. You would use that one for pizza. The machine doesn't actually cook anything; it just kneads and then you take out the pizza dough and bake it in your normal oven. If you aren't making pizza dough, the next selections you'll make are the loaf size and crust type. Once those are chosen, press the "timer" button. Based on your other selections, a time will show up and all you have to do is push "start."

After kneading and before the machine begins baking, many people will remove the dough so they can take out the kneading paddles, since they often make an indent in the finished bread. The paddles should simply pop out or you can buy a special hook that makes the removal easier. Now you can return the bread to the machine. The lid is closed during the baking process. If it's a glass lid, you can actually see what's going on. You'll hear the paddle spinning on the motor, kneading the dough. It lies still for the rising stage, and then starts again for more kneading if necessary. The motor is also off for the proving stage. Next, the heating element switches on, and steam rises from the exhaust vent as the bread bakes. The whole process usually takes a few hours.

There's a lot of work involved in making bread by hand. When you use a machine, that machine does a lot of the busy stuff for you. You just add your dough and the bread maker starts doing its thing, giving you time to do other chores or sit back and relax. As a note, not all bread makers are completely automatic, so if you want this benefit, you'll probably have to pay a bit more money. It's worth it for a lot of people, though.

Lightning Source UK Ltd.
Milton Keynes UK
UKHW051543191220
375378UK00002BA/29